Why a Fragrant Garden?

Rodney Hyett/Dale Harvey

Fragrance is the one element that can add an entirely new dimension to an existing garden. No matter the size or style of garden, strategic placement of fragrant plants can bring a garden to life.

We choose trees in the garden for shade and scale and plant lawn for unity and ease of care. However, think before rushing in to plant the broad canvas of your garden – shrubs, perennials, groundcovers, climbers and pot plants can all be chosen with that added asset of fragrance. Use your nose as well as your eyes in selection.

The placing of just one single Daphne in a pot or courtyard can bring untold pleasure throughout the dormant winter months. Similarly, an arch draped with Wisteria in bloom is one of the delights of spring, the sweet fragrance evoking memories of our grandparents' gardens with their abundance of scented blooms.

Rather than just admire plants for their colour, or appearance, bend over and smell – you could be pleasantly surprised. Often the most gaudy floriferous blooms are totally bereft of fragrance while the more subtle flowers can have the most heady refreshing fragrance.

Once fragrance is part of your life, gardening and plants will never be the same. There will be few scented plants you will be able to walk past without being aware of their added charm.

Flowers are fragrant because it is makes them attractive to their pollinators, whether that be bees, butterflies, wasps, other insects or even birds and other small mammals such as possums. The fragrance is due to volatile oils produced in glands at the base of the petals. Pollinators follow the odour trail these chemicals produce until they can see the flower. Insects have cells in their antennae and feet which are similar, but even more sensitive than those of the human tongue.

A floriferous garden such as this is full of blooms to pick for posies and flower arrangements. The old tradition of messages being conveyed through flowers is a charming, but unfortunately, lost art. Nevertheless, bunches of flowers are always welcomed and convey an image of the garden from which they were picked.

The Language of Flowers

Last century there was an added fascination in receiving a bunch of flowers for the secret message they conveyed. Ardent messages were expressed through the innocent gift of flowers. Traditionally each flower had a meaning and here are just a few:

Almond flower - Hope

Ambrosia - Love returned

Basil - Hatred

Bluebell - Constancy

Cyclamen - Diffidence

Daffodil - Regard

Forget-me-not - True love

Fuchsia - Taste

White jasmine - Amiability

Yellow jasmine - Grace and elegance

Jonquil - Desiring a return of affection

Purple lilac - Constancy

White lily- Diffidence

Yellow lily - Regard

Narcissus - True love

Red rose - Love

Yellow rose - Jealousy

Snowdrop- Consolation

Sweet Pea - Departure and lasting pleasures

Sweet William - Gallantry

Tuberose - Dangerous pleasures

Yellow tulip - Hopeless love

Red tulip - Declaration of love

The AUSTRALIAN Women's Weekly Garden Guides

The Fragrant garden

By Trisha Dixon

A garden alive with flowers and fragrance is surely one of life's great pleasures, for even the most beautiful flowers seem even more enticing when they are perfumed. With this book you can create a scented corner or terrace, a herb ladder, or simply add some fragrance to your existing borders and beds. There's also a practical chart to help you make the right plant choice for your garden. Plan to unearth the extra charm of fragrance in your garden all year round.

Hidden Delights

ragrance is surely the most subtle tool available to the gardener. With it, the gardener may weave a web that enthralls all who visit. For what is more intoxicating than a long forgotten scent stirring memories of the past. The most ordinary garden can be transformed into a romantic idyll with these invisible spirits.

The most powerful of our senses, fragrance adding a new dimension to our appreciation of a garden. It is indeed one of the hidden delights of the garden. It has been said that the fragrance of plants is like an unseen ghost. It sneaks up on you as you round a turn in the garden, before you even see the plant from which it came.

For pure nostalgia, fragrant plants such as lilac, lily of the valley, old roses and Wisteria, have it over the modern hybrids of today. Burying your face in a bunch of violets or an old cabbage rose is akin to inhaling the elixir of life. Invigorating and refreshing to the soul and evocative of youthful memories.

Without fragrance, where is the spirit of the garden? It may be clever in its design, have a bounteous array of colour and blooms, but without the subtlety of fragrance, such a garden is merely a collection of plants.

How enticing on bleak winter days to find in the garden a bloom so precious for its exquisite scent, to go to bed on summer evenings with the fragrance of frangipani drifting through the window, or to have a courtyard filled with the subtle fragrance of just one Gardenia. Why use plants without fragrance! The subtle allure of scent adds another dimension to gardening and plant selection.

Take inspiration from our photographs and garden plans. Begin your fragrant garden in a pot, on an arch, or a in corner. Never again will you walk through a garden without appreciating the beauty fragrance brings to a garden.

A walk through the garden mid-summer reveals the sweet fragrance of the tobacco plant which comes into its own at night when the star-shaped flowers fully open.

The refreshing aroma of eucalyptus from the manna gum fills the air after a shower of rain. The vivid purple of the mint bush behind adds a touch colour and a wonderful minty scent.

The hallmark of a cottage garden is informality - every piece of ground is used. Here, a sundial makes a perfect centrepiece surrounded by heartease, catmint, lavender, and 'The Fairy' roses.

Passers-by are ensured a scent-filled stop in this garden corner. Lavender spills out through the bench slats so that the perfume will be released when the lavender is leaned against.

Fragrant Charms

Unlike any other style of garden, a fragrant garden is simply a garden planted with that added dimension of fragrance. It needn't be smart, large, over the top, native or wild. It can be as simple as a unit with a few windowboxes, a townhouse with a potted courtyard, an inner city terrace with fragrant climbers on the walls, or a vast country garden with scented shrubs and groundcovers at each turn.

Viola 'Purple Robe'

A Romantic Idyll

A fragrant garden is purely what you want and what you can cope with. It only takes a bit of thought when selecting plants. Don't be lured solely by colour. Select those with that extra allure of fragrance, they will repay you tenfold. Pick the flowers for scented posies, fill the house with vases of fragrant blooms and enjoy the added dimension of walking around or working in a scented garden.

Create your own romantic idyll. Use fragrant evergreens to enclose areas and create a sense of mystery and secrecy, use evergreen climbers to camouflage boundaries and sheds, and plant fragrant pathways. Plan your garden as an artist uses a canvas – nothing too tricksy or obvious that will jar the eye. And don't just think of flowers when planning a fragrant garden. Leaves and blooms are well known for being aromatic, but fruit, bark, roots, seed pods, buds and stems can also produce heavenly scents.

What is Fragrance?

Words used to describe scent are quite often inadequate, for who can really describe the ambrosial perfume of Daphne or the delicate perfume of lily of the valley? It is easy to classify colour, but defining fragrance is not as straightforward. Essential oils give plants their fragrance, but how people perceive these is a different matter. What may be tantalising to one, may be overpowering to others. While flowers such as rose, jasmine, violets and eucalypts have distinctive fragrances, others are far more elusive to define.

The climbing rose 'Crimson Glory' is a superb contrast against the white of this archway. Seats on either side allow visitors to linger and enjoy the rich fragrance, which is added to by lush plantings of French lavender and Pelargoniums.

Simon Kenny (Garden at Gledswood, NSW, left)/Dale Harvey

Charming bits of information

I profess to be nothing more than the average gardener, enjoying such useless but charming bits of information as that some butterflies and moths exude the same scent as the flowers they visit; that white flowers are the most numerous among the scented kinds, followed by red, yellow and purple in that order, with blue a very bad fifth; that flowers fertilised by birds have no scent at all, birds being without a sense of smell; that dark-haired people have the most highly developed sense, where as albinos are generally lacking it altogether; that some flowers smell different in the morning from in the evening......

-Vita Sackville-West.

A shrub border of Mexican orange blossom (*Choisya ternata*), yellow broom (*Genista florida*) and native mint bush (*Prostanthera ovalifolia*), top left, is both a colourful and fragrant addition to a garden.
A delight on a warm sunny day, yellow jasmine (*Jasminum humile* 'Revolution') combined with Sweet William, top right, climbing over a trellis fence.
French lavender and climbing old-fashioned roses adorning verandah railings, right, create a fragrant backdrop for this rustic bench.

Fragrant Gardens in History

The tradition of fragrance dates back to the very first gardens – even as far back as the Garden of Eden. Inexorably tied in with religion, cultural rites and superstition, aromatic plants have played an integral role in history. The Egyptians, Greeks and Romans embraced the use of aromatic plants for religious and personal purposes and in the Middle Ages, the use of perfume was believed to be a potent weapon against plagues.

The Ancient Egyptians grew scented plants on the banks of the Nile and imported spices to make unguents (ointments). These were used to scent and soothe their bodies and were also used to embalm them when they died. The Pharoah's Royal Barge was said to have been washed with flower-scented water before it set sail. Phials of perfume entombed with the pharoahs were still fragrant when opened centuries later.

Aromatherapy

The Greeks believed that the soul, like fragrance, entered the body through the nose. They used fragrant plants in aromatherapy and bathing as well as in their study of natural medicine. It was not long before the Romans too, began to appreciate and prize fragrant flowers and expensive perfumes. The Roman Army was said to go into battle with helmets wreathed in roses.

By the Middle Ages, aromatic plants and herbs were greatly valued to counteract infections and diseases and everyone with a garden, however small, grew herbs. Lilies, roses, honeysuckle and herbs were grown in enclosures, similar to the monastery gardens. This was the time of apothecaries and the birth of Physic Gardens.

It wasn't until the 18th century that plant fragrances were classified into categories. Carolus Linnaeus, Swedish naturalist and the father of modern botany, identified these classes: Aromatic, Ambrosial, Alleaceous (garlic-like), Fragrant, Hircine (goat-like), Foul, and Nauseous.

The exciting voyages of discovery that culminated in the settlement of Australia uncovered a wealth of new plant material. Plant explorers were finding a multitude of exotic new plant species and botanists and garden lovers were experimenting with a new palette of plant species.

Wild Gardens

However, this was also the era of the landscape movement – the sweeping lawns and uninterrupted vistas espoused by William Kent and Capability Brown. Flower beds surrounding the stately homes were swept away until the 19th century, when carpet bedding became the vogue. Bright coloured annuals were favoured for brilliant display rather than the old-fashioned perfumed favourites.

Thankfully, cottagers were not overawed by what they saw over their fences and kept to their tapestry of old roses, honeysuckle and fragrant perennials. It was Gertrude Jekyll, following William Robinson's writings and disdaining carpet bedding and promoting the more relaxed form of wild garden, who brought the simplicity and charm of the forgotten cottage garden back into fashion.

In Australia, Edna Walling became one of the most influential voices in landscape style and her love of simple perfumed plants took the imagination of generations of gardeners. Her writings, photographs and landscape designs were published in books, journals and newspapers and today, after her death, continue to be a source of inspiration for many gardeners that favour the romantic style.

It can often be inspiring for new gardeners to visit the gardens of Edna Walling and other great gardening masters. The Open Garden Scheme, which operates in Australia, New Zealand and Britain, organises the opening of hundreds of gardens throughout the year, many planned by garden designers of great renown.

Simon Kenny (Garden at Gledswood, NSW)

Making Plans

There is no set formula when planning a fragrant garden – it can be as simple as a windowbox overflowing with scented geraniums, as vast as a wild country garden or as stylish as a pair of clipped Gardenia in pots. In essence, a fragrant garden is a personal collection of favourite plants, selected with fragrance in mind. Deciding on a style of garden is your first priority as this will often decide the type of plants which are best to grow. Whether your choice is a cottage, formal, Mediterranean, single colour or other style of garden there are a few simple rules to follow.

As with planning any type of garden, first consider the size and aspect of the garden as this will influence the number and variety of plants that can be grown. Choose plants which are suitable for the climate and are practical rather than ones which have great romantic appeal but are difficult to maintain.

Be Practical

If you are starting a garden from scratch, visualise the kind of garden you want. Don't worry about what plant goes where, just concentrate on the overall impression you wish to achieve. Imagine paths, banks of glossy foliage, paved areas and flower beds, then set about writing a list of the plants you would like to include in your garden and tick the ones which are fragrant. Divide the plants into categories such as trees, small shrubs, groundcovers, climbers and then find out all you can about them. Is it evergreen or deciduous, annual or perennial? To what height does it grow? Does it need pruning? Is it fragrant during the day or evening? When does it flower? What is its ideal climate? Does it have other decorative features? Our A-Z of fragrant plants beginning on page 110 will answer many of these questions.

Look at plant combinations in your neighbourhood, the amount of space the plants take up, their foliage, textures and colours. Are they in good health? Choose plants that are successful in your area. If you see a plant growing in a neighbour's garden, ask for a cutting and take it to a garden nursery for identification. Visit a specialist herb or general nursery that has its own display gardens.

Above all, keep it simple, once your garden is established you can add more variety as your interest, and garden, grows.

Simon Kenny (Garden at Gledswood, NSW, below)/Rodney Hyett

A border of purple perennial Asters, Iris, pink penstemons and French lavender lead the eye along the path to a potted bay tree.

Clematis montana subtly frames the timber window of this house, providing fragrance throughout spring. Following flowering, attractive feathery seed heads provide interest throughout summer and autumn.

World Climate Zones

Use this map to locate areas of the world that have a climate similar to your own. Plants from those regions are most likely to be successful in your garden. Plants that suit your climate will thrive while those from a different zone may need coddling and special treatment to survive.

KEY TO MAP

Tundra: Average summer temperature 0-10°C (32-50°F). Very severe winters.

Sub-Arctic: Severe winters. Average temperature above 10°C (50°F) for less than four months.

Cold continental: Rain year-round or dry winters. Average summer temperatures below 22°C (72°F).

Cool continental: Severe winters but warm to hot summers. May be rainy year-round or dry in winter.

Temperate: Cool winters, warm summers. May be rainy year-round or wet in winter.

Subtropical: Cool to mild winters, warm to hot summers. May be rainy year-round or dry in winter.

Mediterranean: Cool to mild winters, warm to hot summers. Summers always dry.

Semi-arid plains: Relatively low rainfall which may be seasonal or evenly spread. Cold, cool or mild winters.

Desert: Very low rainfall. Winters may be cold or mild.

Tropical: Year- round warmth above 18°C (64°F). High rainfall, heaviest in summer; winters may be dry or less wet.

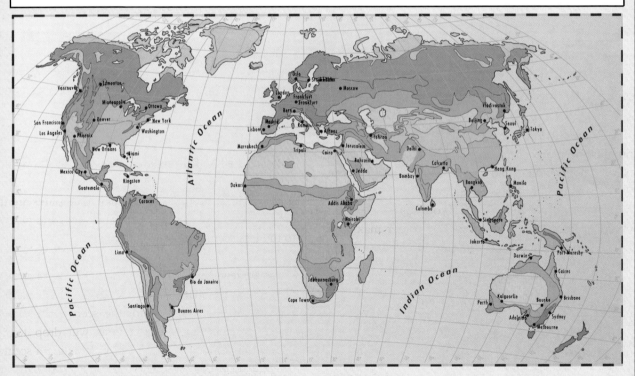

Our terms defined:

RAIN:
Includes snowfalls.

COLD:
Where average temperatures in winter are always below 0°C (32°F).

COOL:
Where average temperatures in winter are between 0°-7°C (32°- 45°F).

MILD:
Where average temperatures in winter are above 0°-7°C (32°F).

WARM:
Where average temperatures in summer are below 20°C (68°F).

HOT:
Where average temperatures in summer are above 20°C (68°F).

The Heide Kitchen Garden is full of perennials, herbs and old-fashioned roses that have been selected for their hardiness and suitability to the cool climate experienced in Victoria, Australia.

Consider Your Site

The choice of plants is determined by the climate, soil and the position you put them in. You can improve the soil by adding mulches, manures, fertilisers and the like. Make sure that the soil pH suits the plants you are wanting to grow. Many nurseries will test the pH for you and advise on whether lime is required to lessen soil acidity. At the other end of the scale, if the soil is too alkaline it may require sulphur or iron sulphate to make it more acidic. Lime may be a useful addition but it doesn't suit all plants; lavenders like it, Magnolias don't as they prefer an acid soil. If your soil isn't suitable for the plants you want to grow, consider making a special bed for them filled with the soil they need.

Plants from different climate zones have evolved to suit that zone. Some cold climate plants suffer greatly if grown in a warmer climate. Likewise, plants that have adapted themselves to dry conditions might die if planted in a wet position. Some plants needs lots of sunlight to thrive while others are scorched by too much sun (see our suggestions for fragrant plants for sun and shade on page 62). There are plants that only develop their full colour if they are exposed to direct sunlight, if planted in the shade, their colour will dull.

If you are unsure seek advice from staff at a local garden nursery. Don't be afraid to ask lots of questions.

Select plants that flower in different parts of the garden throughout the year and provide continuous fragrance, rather than an abundance in spring and summer and a dearth in autumn and winter.

Much of the skill in planning a fragrant garden is in placing plants where they can be enjoyed to most advantage: wintersweet and lavender near a garden entrance, groundcovers to walk on, such as lemon-scented thyme and pennyroyal among stepping stones, paving in a courtyard or on a patio.

Lingering Fragrance

Pastel and white flowers are among the most fragrant, with orange and scarlet shades providing more colour than fragrance. In order of potency, pale pinks are the most scented, moving through the mauves and yellows to the less scented purples and blues.

Not all scented plants are brazen with their gifts. There are few plants whose scent really fills the air with fragrance and many need to be brushed past or brought close to the face for the scent to be experienced. Some fragrant leafed trees will drop foliage where it is trodden into the ground creating a scented covering, e.g. Lemon-scented gum (*Eucalyptus citriodora*) while other plants benefit from the close of day, becoming more fragrant after the sun has set.

One design aspect that can favour the use of fragrance is hedging and windbreaks that will create pockets of still air on which the fragrance can linger. Aromatic conifers or scented Viburnums can be used as windbreaks and low-growing hedges of lavender, rosemary or roses, such as 'Stanwell Perpetual', add fragrance, structure, interest and colour to the garden.

A walk through the garden mid-summer will reveal many fragrant delights such as the sweetly scented tobacco plant (*Nicotiana*) which really comes into its own at night when the star-shaped flowers, in shades of white, green, pink and yellow, open fully. Positioned near a pathway, its scent is taken in by all passers-by.

Summer Fragrance

Lavender is a feature of the summer garden and will flower through the driest, hottest summer without even looking like wilting! This species, *Lavandula stoechas*, self-seeds prolifically.

Memories are so often linked with fragrances and those that linger in our mind are frequently associated with the heady days of summer – those long evenings when time seems to stand still. No frantic rushing to meet appointments, long and leisurely meals outdoors to capture the evening breeze and the poignancy of those special night-time scents.

Temperate climate gardens can grow such treasures as the orange jessamine (*Murraya paniculata*), a large shrub with the most richly scented, beautifully white, single flowers which cluster at the ends of the branches throughout summer. Evergreen and with colourful large red berries in winter, it makes the ideal screen plant or tall hedge.

Exotic Delights

Another favourite for warm, humid climates is the frangipani (*Plumeria rubra*), a shapely deciduous tree with richly scented waxy flowers on show all summer. Like the jessamine, the frangipani won't tolerate frost or cold winds, preferring a warm, humid climate with good drainage. Although exotic in both appearance and perfume, the frangipani can be easily propagated and even large branches can be struck from cuttings.

An understated plant, but one of the most refreshingly fragrant of all plants is the lemon verbena (*Aloysia triphylla*). The best places to look for this shrub is an old-fashioned plant nursery or herb or cottage garden specialist. A deciduous bushy shrub, it has fairly insignificant sprays of white or pale purple flowers in

15

summer, but the most evocative of lemon scents. Use the leaves for summer drinks, in your tea or dry the leaves to make sachets for the linen cupboard.

From the Australian rainforests, comes the native frangipani (*Hymenosporum flavum*), a member of the Pittosporum family, which contains many other fragrant specimens. An evergreen tree with richly perfumed, creamy yellow flowers, it is capable of scenting an entire garden. These fast growing trees, which don't like frost, will reach 10-15m (30-50ft) and need good moisture and mulch. Yellowing in new leaves is caused by iron deficiency and can be corrected by a dose of iron chelates.

A Summer Favourite

Many gardeners regard lavender as their favourite of the summer-flowering plants and there are some 25 varieties from which to choose. Lavenders range from the unusual green lavender, *Lavandula viridis*, to the white, *L. angusti-folia* 'Alba', from the pink form, 'Rosea' to the woolly lavender, *L. lanata*, dwarf, 'Munstead', and semi-dwarf 'Hidcote'. As well there is Italian lavender, *L. stoechas,* (regarded as a noxious weed in some areas so it needs to be grown with care), and English, *L. angustifolia*. The best-known, French lavender (*L. dentata*), has toothed green foliage and lavender-blue flowers. See the "Cottage Charm" chapter beginning on page 74 for more details about lavender.

Lavender needs full sun, good drainage, pruning, as well as the addition of lime in autumn and a small amount of fertiliser in spring. Lavender will tolerate drought conditions, needing little water once the roots have been established in the ground. To keep lavender from becoming straggly and too woody, prune after flowering. This will keep lavender bushes in good shape and encourage foliage growth and better blooms the following year. Think of all the lavender bags or potpourri that can be made with the fragrant harvest! See our ideas on page 80.

The Christmas or Easter lily (*Lilium longiflorium*) (1) is the most beautiful of the Lilium family with its stately fragrant blooms. It needs filtered sun and can be grown in a pot or in the open garden. The rich honey scent of the honeysuckles (2) are an integral part of the summer garden. They are wonderful instant cover-ups for unsightly sheds or fences, and are easily grown from cuttings. An underrated shrub, the sometimes ungainly appearance of lemon verbena (3) belies the presence of its deliciously scented foliage. The leaves are a zesty addition to teas, potpourris, and herb sachets. There are a number of shrubby sages (Salvias) (4) which can be used for screening fences or hiding unattractive garden fixtures. Boasting more than 700 species the therapeutic properties of the plant are well known; sage is reputed to give long life to those who use it; hence its name Salvia which translates as salvation.

The Australian native frangipani with its yellow, heavily perfumed flowers is one of summer's star performers. A tall, quick growing tree, it is not suited to areas which experience heavy frosts.

Autumn Fragrance

Fragrance is overlooked in this season of tawny leaves and hues of gold through to crimson, but there are a surprising number of scented plants to add cheer to the disarray of fallen leaves. Many perennials, annuals and roses continue flowering well into winter, or until the first frosts in cooler climate gardens. Fragrant foliage also continues to scent gardens.

Fragrant roses that bloom throughout autumn include the delicate pink semi-double 'Souvenir de St Anne's', the shell-pink hybrid musk, 'Felicia', the almost magenta-pink bourbon 'Madam Isaac Pereire', the thornless climber 'Zéphirine Drouhin' and the soft pink 'Stanwell Perpetual' which flowers well into winter.

Autumn-flowering bulbs include the strongly scented belladonna lily (*Amaryllis belladonna*), which needs a sunny well-drained position, the tuberose (*Polianthes tuberosa*), the first of the jonquils and the most beautiful of all Irises, the china blue stylosa (*Iris unguicularis*), a beardless Iris with a long-tubed flower and narrow leaves.

Colour and Scent

While this is the season that many shrubs lose their leaves in full autumn glory, there are a number that can be planted for their fragrant flowers rather than colourful foliage. These include *Clerodendrum trichotomum*, a bushy shrub with clusters of tubular white flowers and *C. bungei* which has clusters of red-purple to rosy-pink flowers. Another plant that can last until autumn is Spanish broom (*Spartium junceum*), with its mass of fragrant pea-like yellow flowers and dark green stems, and *Viburnum farreri*, a mass of colour with leaves which turn to a rich red in autumn, and pale-pink flowers which bloom from autumn into winter and are then followed by bright red berries.

Osmanthus heterophyllus is quite a rare shrub, but one worth tracking down for its amazingly scented white flowers borne freely throughout autumn. It is an evergreen upright shrub with handsome foliage resembling holly leaves, growing to 2-3m (6-10ft) in height. It is a really treasured plant.

Rodney Hyett/Leigh Clapp/Andre Martin

The autumn flowers of the rose 'Madame Issac Pereire' (1) are quite stunning with their rich fragrance and old-fashioned form. This Bourbon rose can be grown as a large bush or climber. What could be more charming than a mass of heartsease (*Viola tricolor*) (2), spilling out of a tub sited near the front or back door. These little wild pansies self-seed readily and will fill in bare spots in the garden without becoming too invasive. They flower from spring through to autumn.

Spanish broom (*Spartium junceum*) (3) has a long-flowering period with its mass of highly fragrant yellow pea-like flowers on show from late spring through to autumn. Much of the art of garden design is in creating pleasing tapestries of colour, whether in foliage or flowering plants. Here, the use of the fragrant flowering Spanish broom lends vivid highlights to this area.

Cherry pie, or Heliotrope, (*Heliotropium arborescens*) (4) is an evergreen, bushy shrub with scented violet-coloured flowers that bloom from late spring into autumn. Cherry pie is particularly favoured for these highly scented blooms which grow in dense clusters. Particularly fast growing, it should be tip pruned regularly to prevent it becoming leggy; it is frost tender.

Stocks (*Matthiola incana*) can be sown in autumn for some winter colour.

Joe Filshie

AUTUMN-WINTER
fragrance and colour garden

This small space is a place of rest, a place to withdraw, relax, take in the colours of autumn and enjoy the fragrance. A circular pond provides a point of reflection and waterlilies play on its surface and produce a gentle scent.

The garden is dominated by eight crepe myrtles, which flower into autumn and offer a delicate scent. The flowers provide the garden with bright colour, and as the trees are deciduous, they will allow the sun to come through during the winter months.

The perimeter of the circle is adorned with scented groundcovers such as catmint, violets and a selection of fragrant annuals, such as stocks or dwarf sweet peas. The crepe myrtles are underplanted with Daphne. Scented foliage plants such as diosma and the grey honey myrtle follow the circular paving, providing a soft texture and different shades of green.

The timber arbor is softened by the Azors jasmine, while the Gordonia provides a contrasting textured backdrop to the garden. Its large white flowers with yellow centres add interest to the foliaged green wall. Either side of the arbor is framed by sweet olive, an evergreen shrub which produces a wonderful heady scent, especially in the evenings.

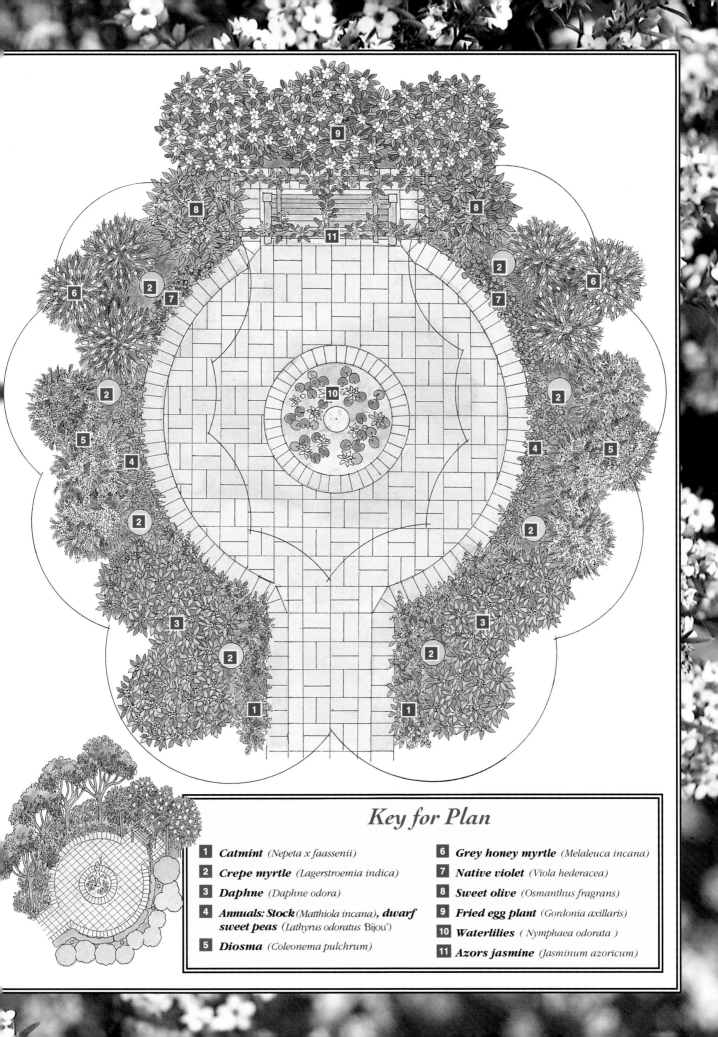

Key for Plan

1 **Catmint** (*Nepeta x faassenii*)

2 **Crepe myrtle** (*Lagerstroemia indica*)

3 **Daphne** (*Daphne odora*)

4 **Annuals: Stock** (*Matthiola incana*)**, dwarf sweet peas** (*Lathyrus odoratus* 'Bijou')

5 **Diosma** (*Coleonema pulchrum*)

6 **Grey honey myrtle** (*Melaleuca incana*)

7 **Native violet** (*Viola hederacea*)

8 **Sweet olive** (*Osmanthus fragrans*)

9 **Fried egg plant** (*Gordonia axillaris*)

10 **Waterlilies** (*Nymphaea odorata*)

11 **Azors jasmine** (*Jasminum azoricum*)

Winter Fragrance

Fragrance is one of the winter gardener's untold delights – for what could be more inducive to venturing outside than the inviting fragrance of wintersweet or Daphne on the air? It is all the more precious during these cold months as the garden slumbers in its winter dormancy.

Winter-flowering plants tend to be more subtle and discreet than those flowering later in the year. Apart from the brilliant golden wattle blooms of Cootamundra (*Acacia baileyana*), and Queensland silver wattle (*A. podalyriifolia*), most fragrant winter plants are demure yet so pure and exquisite in their own modest way. As the garden is not a mass of blooms, all the more reason to select special fragrant plants to enjoy mid-winter.

Powerfully Fragrant

The Australian native Boronia is rated one of the world's most fragrant plants and has a sweet citrus-like fragrance. If you only have room for one, try the highly fragrant brown variety, *Boronia megastigma* or the delicate lime-yellow flowered *B. megastigma* 'Lutea'. They can be tricky to grow and require sandy, acid, well-drained soil that is moist, with a cool root run. All Boronia species will benefit from flower pruning.

One Shakespeare's woodbine, the winter honeysuckle (*Lonicera fragrantissima*), is enough to scent an entire garden. Flowering on bare twigs, there is nothing startling in the pale blooms apart from the most overpoweringly beautiful fragrance. This favourite of the old-fashioned garden has the sweetest of citrus scents. A tall shrub, growing to 2.5m (8ft), it is almost

The brown Boronia (*Boronia megastigma*), is grown by perfume makers for its unforgettable fragrance. Grow in sandy, acid soil and prune flowers to promote further blooms.

deciduous in cool climates but keeps its leaves in warmer areas and grows in well-drained or moist soil in sunny or semi-shaded areas.

Wintersweet or allspice, (*Chimonanthus praecox*) is a must-have for the winter garden with its translucent blooms of the most delicate yet powerful fragrance. It is reasonably frost hardy but in a cold area it needs to be grown in a sheltered position such as a north- or west-facing wall or fence. One sprig in a vase will fill a room with its heady aroma. It has demure looking wax-like blooms on bare branches and grows into a shrub to 2m (6ft) in height. Wintersweet needs cool to mild winters and can take years to flower.

Clusters of Buds

Another oddity of the winter garden is the Chinese witch hazel (*Hamamelis mollis*), with its yellow tassel balls of flowers, quite unlike any other bloom. Appearing on bare stems, the flowers are bright yellow and highly fragrant. Deciduous shrub to 3m (10ft) high.

Viburnums are becoming increasingly popular, and with 120 species and even more named varieties, there are many from which to choose. *Viburnum x burkwoodii* is a favourite with its cluster of pink buds transforming into fragrant balls of white. Grows to 3m (10ft) high.

Viburnum carlesii is also particularly fragrant with rounded heads of white-flushed pink flowers in late winter followed by decorative black fruit on a dense deciduous shrub that grows to 1.5m (5ft).

Two native plants that provide fragrance and blooms throughout winter are the Banksias and the wattles. Look out for the coast Banksia (*Banksia*

Jonquils are one of the first indicator's that the garden is awakening. Their sweet scent and cheerful flowers are are all the more endearing as they bloom during the months when so many plants lie dormant.

The silver wattle (*Acacia dealbata*), is covered with bright yellow fragrant blooms from winter into spring. With more than 750 species of Acacias from which to choose, there are ones to suit most environments. All are quick growing and evergreen, prefer full sun and will survive in the poorest soils.

integrifolia) which attracts birds to its flowers, and heath Banksias (*B. ericifolia*), which require a sunny position and well-drained soil. Among the wattles, the white sallow wattle (*Acacia floribunda*) and silver wattle (*Acacia dealbata*) provide special winter fragrance and colour.

Honeyed Daphnes

No winter garden would be complete without one of the Daphnes – their scent is so keenly appreciated on the chilly air. Their fragrance is heavy enough to perfume an entire courtyard or fill a small garden. Frustrating plants to grow, at their peak they are just as likely to develop a death wish that will succeed no matter how much coddling and nurturing is given. Main requisites are morning sun, acid soil (no lime), good drainage (as root rot is a common problem) and thorough watering. They prefer a sheltered position with sun or partial shade. The soil may need iron sulphate or sulpher added if it is alkaline to begin with. Sprinkle a small handful of Epsom Salts if the leaves start to yellow. The most delicately scented *Daphne odora* 'Marginata', a small shrub with fragrant purplish-pink or white flowers, and *Daphne mezereum,* which has deep pink to purple flowers followed by red fruits, are lovely garden additions.

Daphnes are a delight to pick on cold days, to bring into a warm room where the honeyed smell is a reminder of the bees and breeze of summer.

Equally as heartbreaking as the Daphnes are the Luculias. *Luculia grandiflora* and *L. gratissima* are evergreen shrubs but they are susceptible to frosts. Their heads of fragrant pink and white flowers appear in mid-winter and continue well into spring.

Banksia 'Giant Candles' performs throughout the winter months. This tall, evergreen, rounded shrub enjoys a warm position in sandy acid soil.

Sweet Daphne (*Daphne odora*), is the most treasured of winter-flowering shrubs. Its intensely fragrant blooms will scent an entire courtyard or a small garden.

Viburnum x burkwoodii is a large semi-evergreen shrub with highly fragrant balls of white flowers which begin in late winter and continue flowering well into spring.

Freesias have a long flowering season and come in a myriad of colours. Their dainty blooms make them a popular bulb for naturalising under the canopy of trees.

The beautifully scented stock (*Matthiola incana*) is treasured for its spicy fragrance and colourful show throughout the coldest months of the year.

Rodney Hyett (Garden of Wirruna Nursery, Vic.)

Buddleia alternifolia is an attractive arching shrub or weeping tree with clusters of fragrant lilac-coloured flowers in early summer.

Spring Fragrance

The whole garden seems to be full of fragrance, bees and blooms in this abundant season. Roses jostle with mock orange, Clematis with Wisteria and violets with lily of the valley, for their chance to be noticed. With so many plants having such fragrant blooms, it's hard not to cast a critical eye over other plants for display only as they don't evoke quite the same response as that of fragrant ones.

Bursting into Bloom

The lilacs are the plants that I most associate with early spring. Their limbs are laden with lilac or white blooms and their fragrance wafts through the air. Although they don't have a long flowering period, they are handsome bushes and the leaves turn a rich autumn hue. Exceptionally hardy, they do require a cool winter to reach their full height of 3-4m (10-13ft). The Persian lilac (*Syringa persica* 'Laciniata') has a more delicate weeping habit and is often found in old cottage or colonial gardens.

And what would spring be without roses – the fragrant climbers, the blowsy old shrub roses, the spicy rugosas, the hybrid teas, the exquisite singles and the oldest of all – the species rose. Transformed from dead looking twigs into the most perfect of all flowers, rose bushes shine during this most abundant of seasons.

The absolutely essential roses for all-round performance, beauty and fragrance include 'Madame Alfred Carrière', an old blush cream rose that keeps on flowering throughout summer and needs lots of room; 'Constance Spry', a beautiful pure pink cupped rose which can be a climber or large shrub; or a rugosa hedge. For pure indulgence, try the single pink blooms of 'Frau Dagmar Hastrup' or the double white of 'Blanc Double de Coubert', or *Rosa filipes* 'Kiftsgate', a rampant climber capable of scaling the tallest tree or covering unsightly fences with its healthy foliage and dainty white blooms.

Don't be without at least one mock orange, (*Philadelphus*) for these shrubs are reputed to have the strongest perfume of any flower. Exquisite in bloom, the mock orange is a deciduous shrub with pure white blooms which grows to around 3m (10ft). Most commonly grown is the *Philadelphus coronarius* with its single white blooms, but try the double white *P.* 'Virginal' or *P.* 'Mexicana' for warmer districts as, although hardy, *Philadelphus* are more suited to cool climates.

Floriferous lilac with its wonderful rich foliage and fragrance is one of the delights of spring and a must-have for old-fashioned gardens.

Mock orange (*Philadelphus*) is one of the most beautiful fragrant plants with its white blooms of such intense fragrance that they are capable of scenting an entire garden when in full bloom.

Persian lilac (*Syringa persica* 'Laciniata') is a deciduous spreading tree with fragrant star-shaped flowers in spring, followed by masses of yellow berry fruit in autumn/winter.

Prickly box (*Bursaria spinosa*) is very thorny, but makes a popular hedging plant with its small shiny leaves and attractive panicles of fragrant blooms followed by brown berries.

Wallflowers (*Cheiranthus cheiri*) have been part of the cottage garden for centuries and are renowned for their fragrance and distinctive warm russet tones. Be sure to choose the older species – the newer cultivars don't have as much fragrance. Keep the plants cut back to prevent them from becoming leggy.

Purple mint bush (*Prostanthera ovalifolia variegatum*), above, is an aromatic shrub associated with the wonderful fragrance of the Australian bush. Its dense mint-scented leaves are almost smothered by a mass of purple flowers during spring. *Clematis Montana Rubra*, top right, is a crowd-stopper in spring with its lightly fragrant star-shaped blooms. Suited to cooler climates, it is among the most popular of all climbers and will cover entire fences, sheds, pergolas or arches.

'Frau Dagmar Hastrup', above, is a rugosa rose with large, single pink fragrant blooms followed by striking red heps that make an interesting autumn/winter display. The fresh green foliage turns a vivid hue during autumn. A good hedging plant. *Wisteria floribunda*, below left, is an aristocratic climber which is magnificent when in flower. Don't be tempted to plant directly onto your house as its eventual weight and climbing habits could bring the house tumbling down over time!

Handsome Hedges

The Buddleias are often referred to as butterfly bushes because their fragrant blooms are favoured by butterflies. Grey-leafed semi-evergreen bushes growing to about 3m (10ft) in height, two fragrant spring flowering species are *Buddleia alternifolia* with its long clusters of lilac-coloured flowers in late spring, and *B. salvifolia* which starts flowering very early in spring. Both species make handsome tall hedges or enclosures. They require well-drained soil and full sun and can be propagated by semi-ripe cuttings in summer.

Anyone that has come across an Osmanthus in flower will not forget the experience. So beautifully fragrant and yet so demure and modest in bloom, the flowers can go almost unnoticed. The scent will lead you to the plant, as its flowers, although daintily pretty, are hidden among the evergreen glossy leaves of this upright shrub. Keep an eye out for *Osmanthus fragrans* with its delicate apricot-scented white blooms.

Seasonal Fragrance

Spring

LILAC *(Syringa vulgaris)* is a mainstay of the country and cottage garden where it has room to spread and its beautifully fragrant panicles of mauve or white flowers scent the entire garden. Deciduous shrub to 5m (19ft). Very hardy and drought-resistant. Prune after flowering. Propagate by softwood cuttings in summer or grafting.

WISTERIA is a heavenly scented climber with long racemes of fragrant mauve or white flowers in spring. Deciduous twining climber, hardy and quick growing. Propagate by grafting or by layering. Plants produced from seed often have poor flowers. Be warned, if close to the house Wisteria can be quite invasive causing damage to drains and foundations as its roots spread.

MELALEUCA is often referred to as paperbark or honey myrtle as there are many species in this group. In common with other family members (Myrtaceae) the fluffy flowers exude a strong honey-like prefume to attract pollinators. Melaleucas are well adapted to poorly drained soils and are easily raised from seed.

Spring
Melaleuca

Leigh Clapp

Summer
Frangipani

Leigh Clapp

Summer

TOBACCO plant *(Nicotiana)* flowers profusely throughout summer with its sweetly scented white or lime green blooms more noticeable in the evenings. Grows easily from seed; spreads and self-seeds readily.

ANNUALS and perennials are suited to growing in rich soil in warm climate gardens. Propagate by seed in spring.

LAVENDER is one of the most popular of all garden flowers with its highly fragrant mauve blooms on display throughout summer. Suitable for hedges, pots or in the general garden (except dense shade). Evergreen small shrubs to 1m (3ft), very hardy. Side dress with lime once a year. Propagate by semi-ripe cuttings in summer.

FRANGIPANI is a favourite of the tropical garden with its deliciously fragrant waxy blooms scenting an entire garden. There are at least 40 different species, however all are frost-tender. Deciduous and evergreen shrubs and trees to 8m (25ft)

Rodney Hyett

Autumn

ROSES are often flowering well into autumn and are all the more treasured as so little is in flower this time of year. Choose wisely, as there are so many to decide between – many are wonderfully scented, particularly the old-fashioned roses. There are deciduous, semi-evergreen or evergreen shrubs and climbing roses. Very hardy and will survive droughts, frost and heat.

GARDENIAS are the prima donnas of the plant world with their elegant pure white sweetly scented blooms cherished for bridal bouquets. Evergreen shrubs and trees, frost tender, growing to 2m (6ft). Keep moist and fertilise each month with acid plant food. Propagate by greenwood cuttings in spring or semi-ripe cuttings in summer.

LEMON-SCENTED GUM (Eucalyptus citriodora) is one of the most stately trees with its highly scented leaves emitting a strong fragrance when crushed, and pure white blossoms heralding the beginning of winter. Evergreen tree to 30m (100ft) with a smooth pale cream trunk.

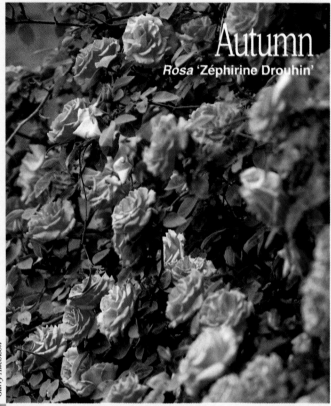

Autumn
Rosa 'Zéphirine Drouhin'

Garry Aitchison

Winter
Daphne

Winter

WINTERSWEET (Chimonanthus praecox) is the treasure of the winter garden with its amazingly sweet blooms appearing throughout the cold winter months. Deciduous shrub, slow growing to 2.5m (8ft). Flowers borne on bare stems.

DAPHNE is wonderful in winter and it is one plant is capable of scenting an entire courtyard or front garden. Don't take them for granted however, as they will not stand neglect. Evergreen, small shrub to 1.5m (5ft), frost hardy. Requires morning sun and slightly acidic soil. Don't allow to dry out. Propagate by semi-ripe cuttings in summer.

JONQUILS and freesias are among the most fragrant of the late-winter to early-spring flowering bulbs and will quickly naturalise in the garden. Bulbs should be planted in autumn and watered during winter for good spring flowering. Propagate by offsets in autumn.

STOCK (Matthiola incana) are rapidly growing annuals renowned for their spicy clove-like fragrance which abounds in winter and early spring. For winter flowering, sow seeds in mid autumn.

David Young/Dale Harvey/Jennie Churchill

Colour Partners

Combining colour and fragrance

Colour is a wonderful tool for creating the mood of a garden – bright colours will invariably create a cheerful atmosphere while the restrained white and green garden imparts an air of elegance. Take into consideration the colour of your house, roof, fence, outbuildings and any other structures and then choose one colour for paths, walls, steps and paving. When choosing colour bear in mind that red will leap out from the background, while blue will recede. For example, if you plant red flowers along the furthest garden fence you'll find that it will appear to reduce the overall size of the garden; a planting of deep blues or purples will appear to increase the space.

Colour can also affect your mood, with blues being calming, while reds and yellows are exciting. Crisp fresh pastel colours highlight spring, vibrant reds and yellows warm up summer, while nautical

Fragrant yellow jonquils with pink azalea 'Magnifica'.

Crisp white and yellow - delicate daisies and yarrow.

A brilliant combination of stocks, poppies and Calendulas.

Vibrant golden poppies in a carpet of heartsease.

blues cool it down; burgundy, orange and golden tones will enhance autumn. Single colour plantings will need careful planning while any number of colours can be combined to create a dramatic effect, such as mixing blue flowers with bright yellow or red with cool greens.

The angle of the sun affects the way we see colour, and as the angle of the sun changes, depending on the hour, the month and the position of your garden, so too will the colours in your garden. Vertical light is harsher and brighter so that pastels may appear washed out under the severe glare of midday sun and only bright colours will remain strong and shine. Horizontal afternoon and morning light accents the subtlety of light, soft colours.

Pleasing Combinations

Develop your own colour scheme with an artist's eye and when visiting gardens, look out for pleasing colour combinations. White and blues will go with most colours and they are a perennial favourite, but oranges and red can be a bit hectic if grown right next to each other – break them up with clumps of greenery or white flowers. Mauve-blues look good with bright pink and delicate yellow blooms.

White gardens are undeniably popular as there is a stylish elegance in a mass of white plants, and they can impart a sense of coolness in a hot climate. White plants can also lighten dark corners, brighten a garden at dusk, make the garden appear larger and create a sense of fullness. Choose a range of white-toned flowers from brilliant white to creamy off-whites as these will blend with the different coloured foliage of each plant. There is also no colour that can possibly clash with white, so it is undeniably safe.

Red adds definition to borders and can also be used for filling spaces or as a complementary colour to yellows, whites and blues. Red flowers can be anything from pale pinks to deep purples and violets. Yellow flowers can be dotted through the garden and will draw the eye from one end of the garden to the other.

A hot dry exposed pocket of your garden could benefit from planting lavenders, rosemary, catmint and olive trees (to provide shade). The grey tones of these plants will blend together to create a Mediterranean theme – add a few pots to complete the effect.

It really boils down to personal taste and the vision you have for your garden. You may like to go back to basics and consult the colour spectrum to see which colours are opposing or complementary. Keep in mind when choosing plants, whatever colour, that there is some fragrance to scent the garden.

The mauve pom-pom heads of chives provide a delicate contrast to their green foliage.

Colourful buds offset the pure white blooms of *Rhododendron* 'Fragrantissimum'.

Jennie Churchill/Rodney Hyett/Joe Filshie

Calming white clusters of diosma.

Cooling blue hues of fluffy Allium heads and larkspurs.

Mexican orange blossom teamed with Babiana.

Pink blooms and grey foliage of Dianthus.

Borderlines

Add interest to your flower borders by including perfumed plants such as lilies, Verbena, stocks, bergamot, Iris, jonquils, polyanthus and violets. Lavender, catmint, candytuft, thyme or clipped box can all be used to add formality to borders.

Dianthus are marvellous border plants with their fragrant blooms throughout spring and neat compact foliage. Thriving in full sun, they prefer a neutral soil pH, but can be difficult to grow in warm, humid conditions. Sprinkle with lime occasionally if your soil is naturally acidic and cut back blooms after flowering. 'Mrs Sinkins' and the clove-scented 'Little Jock' are favourite types of Dianthus.

A Blooming Success

The biggest challenge with a flower border is to have a succession of blooms rather than one grand spring display. Gertrude Jekyll, famous gardener and doyenne of the cottage garden, had the flower border down to a fine art and it is worth seeking out books with her plans and writings for ideas on how to have a succession of blooms and colours throughout the seasons.

Perfect Planning

Rather than planting a border at random, have some scheme in mind or you will soon find tall plants flopping over and smothering low-growing ones. Also lend an eye to shapes. It is always pleasing to have a number of vertical accents such as Christmas lilies or Galtonias to contrast with rounded shapes such as Santolina, sage or clipped box amongst the perennials. Tall flowers – delphiniums, foxgloves and hollyhocks also give the impression of masses of colour.

Using plants with constant foliage is far more rewarding than a bed of annuals for the simple reason that in the dormant season, annuals are here one day and gone the next. If the flower border is large enough, include some fragrant shrubs; see our ideas on page 56.

Borders can benefit from the use of strong and vibrant colours to give a garden shape. Don't be afraid to mix colours, as in the garden, far left, where the mint bush (*Prostanthera ovalifolia*) adds its purple tones to yellow broom (*Genista*) and the delicate white flowers of Mexican orange blossom, (*Choisya ternata*). For a spectacular display, try a border of clove pinks, Dianthus, left.

Dale Harvey/Simon Kenny (Garden of Gledswood Homestead, NSW, right)

A rambling border of thyme, (*Thymus vulgaris*), softens the edges of this old-fashioned country garden. *Dianthus* 'Pike's Pink', furnishes soft colour, while added height and interest is provided by *Rosa* 'Crimson Glory' climbing over an archway. Other choices for borders include catmint, dwarf lavender and candytuft.

Lush clusters of the musk rose 'Cornelia' (1) adorn this trellis. Flowering from summer to autumn, the fragrance is something quite special. To swathe courtyard walls with fragrant climbing roses, fix a trellis to the wall and thread the roses through. A fragrant reading nook (2) is created by placing a seat in the shade of a timber pergola and positioning sweet peas to climb up the poles and climbing roses to clamber over the top.

The size of a garden has no bearing on its appeal. Here, the use of brick paving, steps and a cottage planting of lavender, sweet peas and lamb's ear (3) creates interest in a quiet corner. A grouping of large terracotta pots all filled with the same plant, in this case Gardenia (4), is statement enough for a small garden. The fresh green foliage looks good all year and, when in flower, its rich fragrance can scent an entire garden.

Small Packages

Fragrance in courtyards and corners

Leigh Clapp/Brent Wilson/Don Brice/Dale Harvey

Courtyards are made for fragrance. What better place to plant a scented Daphne or Osmanthus than in an enclosed area where the scent permeates every corner? Fragrance is undeniably heightened in enclosed areas, and a courtyard is the ideal place for growing a succession of scented plants that will provide fragrance throughout the year.

In a small space it's important to go for the best. Opt for plants such as Gardenias with their knock-out scent and exquisite snow white blooms. They will fill your courtyard with fragrance throughout early summer and will continue to flower off and on until

There are few people who will not agree with me that nothing is more delightful than the fresh scent of flowers in the early morning...

A Flower Gardener's Calendar, Mrs Rolf Boldrewood, 1893

winter. Suited for growing in pots or in the ground, their main requirement is plenty of water and fertilising with a general purpose liquid fertiliser once a month. They thrive in hot humid conditions but keep them sheltered from the hot afternoon sun. They will tolerate some filtered shade but will not flower in full shade.

Courtyards provide limited ground space, so make the most of climbing plants to clothe the walls. *Trachelospermum asiaticum* is a self-supporting evergreen climber with beautifully scented creamy white flowers in summer.

If roses are your passion, choose thornless

One floriferous rose such as 'Blush Noisette', top, is enough to take centre stage in a small area. The sweetly clove-scented blooms are produced throughout the season and its almost thornless canes make it the perfect choice for such an area.

climbers such as 'Kathleen Harrop' (shell-pink, sweetly scented, always in flower), 'Zéphirine Drouhin' (fragrant rose pink), 'Madam Sancy de Parabere' (fragrant pink camellia-type blooms – grows in filtered shade), 'Souvenir du Docteur Jamain' (magnificently fragrant deep red roses – also grows in filtered shade) and 'Paul Neyron' (enormous pink fragrant blooms). There are special lead-headed nails with hooks which are invaluable for securing roses or climbing plants to masonry walls in courtyards.

Flowering Shrubs

If there is room, shrubs are invaluable – try to have a succession of flowering shrubs throughout the year. One of the most elegant fragrant performers for a courtyard area is *Azara microphylla*. This vanilla-scented shrub or small tree grows to around 5m (16ft) in height, has tiny glossy dark green leaves and small clusters of fragrant yellow flowers in late winter and early spring.

Evergreen shrubs such as Azara or Daphne will add form to a courtyard garden in the winter months and provide fragrance and blooms both in the courtyard and in flower arrangements inside. Keep shrubs pruned to prevent them becoming woody and leggy. Pruning should be done after the plant has flowered unless the flowers turn into berries.

Potted Perfume

The courtyard is the perfect environment for a mass of pots overflowing with flowers and foliage. Fragrant bulbs such as lilies, jonquils and freesias are ideal, but don't neglect perfumed foliage plants such as rosemary and lavender. Terracotta pots look wonderful filled with colourful geraniums; the scented leaf varieties make up for unspectacular blooms with a superb range of fragrances. There is every scent from lemon to rose, nutmeg to strawberry. If you want to be practical, too, why not a tub spilling over with herbs; it adds aroma to the courtyard and provides fresh additions and garnishes for lunch or dinner dishes. If space is at a premium consider using wall pots planted with trailing thyme or geraniums.

A outside living area is encircled by a sea of 'Crepuscule', top, a beautifully perfumed rose with few thorns and a long flowering season.
A grouping of pots and a collection of rustic watering cans, centre, makes an interesting garden setting. Fragrant heartsease spill out of pots (and even an old boot), pinks flower in another pot and sweet peas make their way through the foxgloves.
An effective but easy-care garden with lawn and potted plants, left. Lavender, cumquats and rosemary provide fragrance while petunias and Salvias add a splash of colour.

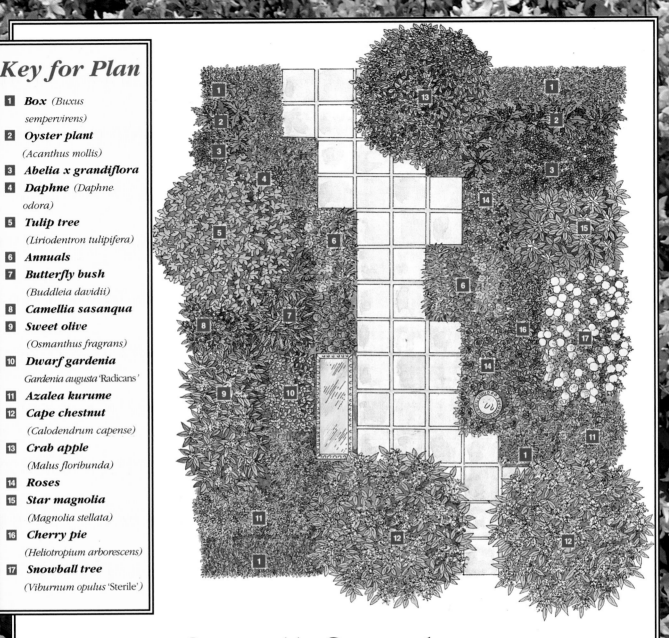

Stroll Garden

The stroll garden is a lovely way to display planting specimens. In this cool climate garden we use a range of species adapted to cooler regions. The entrance to the stroll garden is framed by two cape chestnuts with greyish green foliage and softly scented pink flowers in spring. Kurume azaleas provide a colourful understorey in spring beneath the cape chestnuts. A mixture of beautiful scents created by the Gardenias and sweet olive greet the visitor to the stroll garden while a bird bath attracts birds to enhance pollination. A selection of roses around the bird path provides further perfume and colour. The soft fragrances of Buddleia and cherry pie encourage butterflies to visit. A variety of annuals produce a burst of colour in spring and autumn. Abelia and camellias are great for cut flowers while the oyster plant provides an architectural back drop to the low box hedge. The snowball tree and the star Magnolia enhance the backdrop to the garden. A tulip tree and crab apple also help lead the visitor through the garden.

Tall Orders

Trees with fragrant bark and foliage

Trees provide an important architectural element in a garden, and give a sense of scale while also creating shade – essential to most gardens. While there are many trees with fragrant blooms such as citrus, wattles, frangipanis and Magnolias, there are also many with wonderfully fragrant foliage, such as the eucalypts and balsam poplars. Then there are those with fragrant bark such as the *Magnolia x soulangeana* 'Rustica Rubra' which has lemon-scented bark, and the cinnamon tree *(Cinnamomum zeylanicum)* which yields the spicy scent of cinnamon.

Scented Foliage

Crush a gum leaf in your fingers to evoke the scent of the Australian bush. Eucalypt foliage is often harvested because of the wonderfully potent oils present in the foliage. Two of the most powerfully fragrant are the lemon-scented gum (*Eucalyptus citriodora*) and the peppermint gum (*Eucalyptus nicholii*). Another Australian native with fragrant foliage is the lemon-scented myrtle (*Backhousia citriodora*), a handsome small tree with clouds of lemon-scented white flowers in early summer and wonderful citrus-scented foliage.

The fresh sweet scent of citron is all-pervading in this stunning driveway planted with the lemon-scented gum (*Eucalyptus citriodora*).

Orange trees provide more than just fruit. Their spring blossom is highly fragrant and the aroma of the actual fruit on a warm summer day is sweetly resonant.

Trisha Dixon/ Leigh Clapp/Angus Stewart

The characteristic aroma of the eucalyptus oil of *Eucalyptus mannifera*, right, is prominent in the air after a shower of rain as is the wonderful minty smell of the purple mint bush (*Prostanthera ovalifolia*) in the background. The honey-scented blossoms of the smooth barked apple gum (*Angophora Costata*), above, create a superb display in summer.

The pink Wisteria tree, *Robinia decaisceana*.

Don Brice

An unusual fragrance comes from the pepper tree (*Schinus areira*), often seen in old gardens and along country roads. Its distinctive pink berries are not actually the peppercorns of commerce, although somewhat similar in appearance. The tree grows to around 10–15m (30-50ft) in height and produces delicate weeping branches of fine leaves; it is incredibly hardy and is also drought-resistant. All parts of the tree are fragrant, emitting a spicy aroma.

Flowers and Fruit

The frangipani is considered the most fragrant of all trees with sweetly scented waxy blooms flowering year-round in the right conditions. This is one of the fragrances that really scents the air and entire garden. It's a small tree or large shrub for a warm climate garden.

One of the most underrated but beautiful trees for the garden is the quince which bears wonderful single white blooms, similar to those of a dogwood. It is also the last to lose its foliage in autumn. Its flowers bloom in spring and are followed by a crop of spherical fruits. The fruit hangs on the tree well into winter, and although not eaten fresh, it makes wonderful jellies, pastes and preserves. Planting garlic at the base of the tree is said to improve the flavour of the fruit.

A fast-growing deciduous tree with deliciously fragrant leaves is katsura (*Cercidiphyllum japonicum*). Growing to around 15m (50ft), its round leaves turn a myriad of tawny colours in autumn before dropping. The fragrance from these fallen leaves brings back childhood memories of cooking toffee.

Providing your garden is large enough, grow some tall trees that will really add strength to your overall garden design. So often gardens become filled with smaller flowering trees and the larger picture is overlooked. As well as the eucalypts, the balsam poplars also provide fragrance as well as height. They are remarkably quick-growing as well. *Populus balsamifera* and the black cottonwood, *Populus trichocarpa* are two poplars that emit the resinous fragrance of balsam from their leaves and buds. They are wide spreading trees and need lots of space to grow. Their spreading roots, too, can cause problems if they are planted too close to a house or garden shed.

Dale Harvey

Tree Tips

Trees can absorb inner city noise; reduce glare; provide shade; provide perspective, and purify the air.

However, they can cast too much shade in a small area so that only shade-loving plants will grow. Expensive removal costs can ensue if the tree grows too big for the space and the roots may cause problems with drains.

In small spaces consider planting trees in pots; citrus, Michelia doltsopa, and crepe myrtles grow well in containers.

In a larger courtyard one tree is probably enough, otherwise they tend to dominate the space, a luxury that can only be afforded in a huge rambling garden.

Correct planting is vital for tree establishment. Dig a large hole (square, not round) three times larger than the pot. Mix a handful of blood and bone, bucket of peat moss and bucket of compost and mix with soil at the bottom of the hole. Plant tree, press in firmly, and soak thoroughly. Mulch well to maintain moisture.

An effective screening plant, Cape virgilia, (*Virgilia capensis*) is a fast growing small tree. Fragrant pea-like blooms are borne throughout summer into autumn and the foliage is fern-like and attractive. Like many rampant growing trees, it is short lived and has a life span of about 10 years.

RIGHT: Main and inset: The romatic Magnolia 'Heaven Scent' is an early flowering Magnolia, adding colour and fragrance in spring. Like all Magnolias, it prefers an acid soil (no lime!) enriched with an acidic compost such as leaf mould, and a sheltered aspect. Many others such as *Magnolia grandiflora*, *Magnolia liliflora*, and *Magnolia denudata* would be fragrant additions to your garden.

Dale Harvey

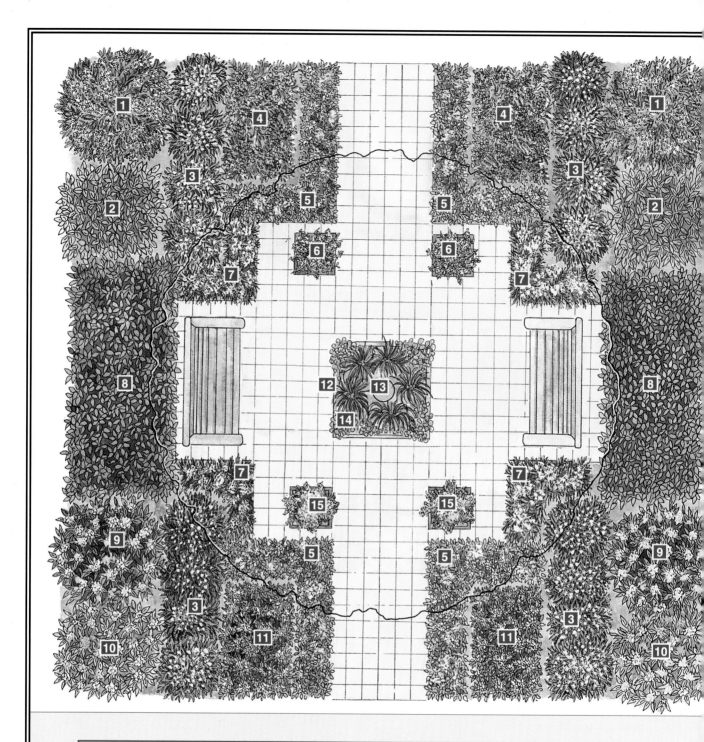

Key for Plan

1 *Lemon-scented tea tree* (Leptospermum petersonii)

2 *Blueberry ash* (Elaeocarpus recticulatus)

3 *Native wax flower* (Eriostemon myoporoides)

4 *Native mint bush* (Prostanthera ovalifolia)

5 *Myrtle* (Myrtus communis)

6 *Lemon-scented myrtle* (Darwinia citriodora)

7 *Weeping baeckea* (Baeckea linifolia)

8 *Lilly pilly hedge* (Acmena smithii)

9 *Lemon ironwood* (Backhousia citriodora)

10 *Aniseed myrtle* (Backhousia anisata)

11 *Coastal rosemary* (Westringia fruticosa)

12 *Spiny mat-rush* (Lomandra longifolia)

13 *White cedar* (Melia azederach)

14 *Native violet* (Viola hederacea)

15 *Homoranthus*

Australian Courtyard

Our indigenous flora has often been neglected in the design of formal gardens. Here is an example where the potential of this flora can be explored. The focal point of this courtyard is a white cedar tree. As a deciduous tree it will allow sun to penetrate the courtyard in winter and provide cooling shade in summer. The delicate foliage and sweet smelling mauve flowers in early spring provide a wonderful canopy under which to sit.

Much of this garden is formally clipped. A low hedge of myrtle guides you into the space, while larger hedges of coastal rosemary and native mint bush enhance the formal entrances. On both sides of the entrance square, terracotta pots house two Australian natives with beautiful aromatic foliage, the lemon-scented myrtle (*Darwinia citriodora*) and Homoranthus. These are clipped into neat ball shapes. A clipped hedge of lilly pilly produces a green wall behind the wooden benches. Their sweet cream flowers and pink fruit provide year-round interest. The rest of the species are allowed to take on their natural shape. These other species include the weeping baeckea (*Baeckea linifolia*), the lemon-scented tea tree and the aniseed myrtle. Two of the corners of the courtyard are highlighted with the blueberry ash, which bears flowers with the scent of licorice.

Myrtaceae - The myrtle family

The myrtle family (Myrtacae) has about 3000 members (species) which are found on every continent but are particularly common in Australia, where the genus eucalyptus dominates the landscape. The leaves of plants in the myrtle family are usually tough and leathery and are characteristically dotted with oil glands which can be readily seen when the leaves are held up to the light. These glands contain volatile oils, which have an odour particular to the species. Eucalyptus oil has a smell familiar to people the world over and is important as a food flavour and also for its medicinal properties. Cloves (and clove oil) are derived from Syzigium aromaticum (Eugenia caryophyllata). The list of plants from this family, which can be used to provide fragrance in the garden, is seemingly endless and here are but a few:

- **Leptospermum petersonii:**
  lemon-scented tea tree
- **Eucalyptus citriodora:**
  lemon-scented gum
- **Backhousia citriodora:**
  lemon ironwood
- **Backhousia anisata:**
  aniseed myrtle
- **Chamelaucium uncinatum:**
  Geraldton wax
- **Darwinia citriodora:**
  lemon-scented myrtle
- **Melaleuca alternifolia:**
  paperbark
- **Baeckea camphorata:**
  camphor-scented baeckea

Romantic Roses

Glorious flowers and fragrance

Few plants conjure up such notions of fragrance as old-fashioned roses. In fact, it seems almost inconceivable that such an object of beauty could be entirely without scent. However, in the rush to breed larger, gaudier blooms, this most enigmatic quality of all can be overlooked.

Generous Fragrance

The true rose scent belongs to the old roses – roses such as the cabbage rose (*Rosa centifolia*), the damask rose (*Rosa damascena*) and the French rose, (*Rosa gallica*). Many of the hybrid perpetuals have inherited this scent, and to a lesser degree, so have the hybrid teas. Within the rose family there are many other scents – musk: 'Penelope', sweet: 'Madam Alfred Carriere', lemon: 'Madame Hardy', raspberry: 'Honorine de Brabant' or clover: 'Fritz Nobis'.

While most old roses are wonderfully generous with their fragrance, there are some that also exude fragrance from their foliage, such as the briar rose (*Rosa eglanteria*) with its green apple fragrance, and *Rosa primula*, with its highly aromatic small leaves and quaint single pale yellow blooms. Some of the most hardy fragrant roses include the following:

- *Albertine*
- *Constance Spry*
- *Cornelia*
- *Fantin Latour*
- *Felicia*
- *Gertrude Jekyll*
- *Souvenir de la Malmaison*
- *Zéphirine Drouhin*

The robust climber 'Lamarque', right, with its tea-scented white blooms is echoed by the lupins beneath and the standard 'Grüss an Aachen' roses in the forground.
'Bonica', above left, a hardy disease resistant rose, is an ideal choice for a hedge with its spreading, arching growth, mass of blooms and abundant orange heps.
The impressively fragrant, deep-pink blooms of 'Bourbon Queen', above right, are on display in summer. This tall, sturdy climber would be perfect adorning a pergola.

Rodney Hyett/Leigh Clapp/Garry Aitchison

Attar of Roses

While the recuperative power of rose petals was known to the Romans, it was only 300 years ago that it was discovered how to make pure attar of roses – the world's most expensive perfume. It takes over 100,000 roses to produce just one ounce – no wonder that small containers are insured for untold thousands.

❖

Rosa damascena trigintipetala, while not a startling rose in appearance, is grown in the Kazanlik Valley in Bulgaria for the sole purpose of making attar of roses. The roses were bought from Damascus by the Turks when they conquered Bulgaria in the 1300s. The roses are harvested before daylight, before the sun dries the petals, and the petals are then boiled to remove the essence. No other country has been able to duplicate this unique essence.

Therapeutic properties
of fragrant plants

Bay
(Laurus nobilis)

Bay leaves beneath the pillow are effective against insomnia and may be used in sachets, potpourri and cushions, steeped in hot water or vinegar as a bath additive or, of course, used in cookery. An inhalation may be used to clear a headache due to blocked nasal passages. One of the more recent findings in herbal medicine research points to the use of oil of bay in stress management, for the scent has been shown to actually lower blood pressure and induce feelings of relaxation.

Chamomile
(Anthemis nobilis)

The tiny, daisy-like blossoms of this fragrant European herb are rich in azulene, a blue oil that soothes skin irritations and promotes healing. A soothing oil is sold which is made from the flowers and leaves. This may be used for accelerating wound healing, treating burns and bruises, earache, neuralgia and toothache. Chamomile is also an ingredient in hair rinses and conditioners; it is particularly effective when mixed with rosewater. Chamomile tea and/or an oil made by steeping dried flowers in a fine carrier oil, such as apricot kernel oil, are particularly useful for those suffering from dandruff. Brew the dried or fresh flowers in the same way as ordinary tea; sweeten with honey, don't add milk. Herbalists say chamomile tea can be used to soothe frazzled nerves and treat menstrual cramps and digestive upsets. Chamomile has a calming effect, and a very, very weak tea has been suggested for a baby with colic.

Tip: Add a strong brew of chamomile tea to warm bath water for a soothing effect on dry or sunburned skin and an overall feeling of calm.

Eucalyptus
(Eucalyptus globulus)

Eucalypts are among the most aromatic plants in the world and the volatile oil, known as eucalyptol, given off by the leaves has powerful healing, disinfectant and antiseptic properties. Eucalyptus oil is useful for all cold conditions related to the respiratory tract, such as coughs, asthma and bronchitis, and may be taken in inhalations, where 6 to 12 drops are put in a bowl of boiling water for steaming. It is also used as an ingredient in throat lozenges. A massage oil with a few drops of eucalyptus oil added will relieve joints afflicted with gout or rheumatism.

Tip: Add a few drops of eucalyptus oil to a bath. It is warming and stimulating and will disinfect any cuts or sores and get rid of offensive body odours.

Fennel
(Foeniculum vulgare)

Fennel is a digestive herb and has been widely used for centuries to alleviate colic and flatulence. The seeds may either be chewed, or made into a tea by infusing 1 to 2 teaspoons of the bruised seeds in 1 cup of boiling water. Steep for 10 minutes and drink the mixture up to three times a day. Infusions of fennel have also been successfully used as a cooling eyewash for tired and inflamed eyes. To make the eyewash, use the same method as above (allowing the mixture to cool, of course). You can either simply bathe the eyes with the liquid or dip squares of clean cloth and place the lukewarm pads over the eyes for 15 minutes.

Barbara Rodanska

Lavender
(Lavandula angustifolia)

Lavender's soothing, antiseptic and anti-inflammatory properties mean this well-loved flower may be also used to make a variety of natural beauty aids and remedies. Try a few drops of lavender oil in the bath to heal skin troubled by a rash. Lavender oil helps to regenerate skin cells and so is excellent for burns – especially sun-burn – and for chapping. By balancing the activity of the sebaceous glands, products containing lavender oil or essence will also tone oily skin and help to treat acne. Well known as a headache herb, lavender can be made into a weak tea (1 teaspoon of dried herb to 500ml hot water). The resulting tea may be dabbed on the temples and forehead or used as a refreshing facial rinse.

Marigold
(Calendula officinalis)

Marigold vinegar is a lovely natural beauty tonic. Combine cider vinegar with a handful of marigold flowers and heat till simmering. Remove from heat, cover and steep overnight, strain. Add 1/2 a cup to a bath for a healing and skin-soothing effect. This is particularly good for a very dry or chapped skin.

Marjoram
(Origanum spp)

Marjoram tea has a soothing and calming effect on the nerves, while the essential oil has mild antiseptic and tonic properties. Contemporary herbalists recommend the tea as a digestive aid. The strongly aromatic oil may be added to a massage oil and used as a warming rub for muscular aches.

Tip: New information suggests that essential oil of marjoram may be used to reduce the spread of fungal and viral disorders, in much the same way as tea-tree oil.

Mint
(Mentha spp.)

Ending a meal with a sprig of mint helps the digestion and sweetens the breath; this very ancient custom culminated in the widespread popularity of 'after dinner mints'. Different fresh mints may be used to scent bathwater.

Rose
(Rosa spp)

Rose leaves are a good substitute for tea, the hips can be made into a delicious conserve or syrup, while the petals are useful as both a medicine and cosmetic. Essential oil of rose is soothing and antiseptic; aromatherapists use it as a sedative and antidepressant.

Rosemary
(Rosmarinus officinalis)

A tea made from fresh rosemary is beneficial for headaches and it is also an excellent digestive aid. Rosemary oil is an effective inhalant and decongestant. Add a few drops to a tablespoon of a carrier oil like sweet almond, and rub on a child's chest to ease a cough. Use rosemary as a rinse for oily hair and skin to remove excessive oil secretions and promote thicker hair.

Thyme
(Thymus vulgaris)

Thyme oil is an indispensable ingredient in many household staples. An infusion of fresh or dried thyme is a good general tonic. Thyme tea is helpful for patients with a cough or cold, while German research has found that inhalations of thyme oil have considerable benefit in loosening phlegm and relaxing the respiratory tract.

Tip: Add 1/2 a teaspoonful of essential oil of thyme to 1 cup of warmed olive oil and use as a stimulating rub for hair and scalp problems. This natural remedy is particularly useful in cases of persistent dandruff and flaking scalp.

by Pamela Allardice

A mixture of fragrant plants adds colour and character to a courtyard garden while providing a variety of flavour for cooking. Mint, parsley, lettuce and strawberries will all grow profusely when planted in pots. Here, star jasmine (*Trachelospermum jasminoides*) climbs from a pot to the window ledge allowing its fragrant aroma to waft through the house.

White orchids, top, (*Dendrobium falcorostrum* '*Alba*'), tumble from a decorative painted pot. This hardy, easy-to-grow plant has a sweet honey perfume. In cooler climates try potting Carter's navel orange, above, and keep it inside, preferably in a conservatory, to ensure an abundance of fragrant blooms, good pollination and sweet fruit.

Jennie Chrucbill

Potted Scents

Pretty and portable packages

The advantage of the potted garden is that those plants performing seasonally can take centre stage. A range of displays can be created by rotating pots in a garden. Try a Daphne or Boronia by the door during winter, mock orange and jonquils in spring, Gardenias and lavender in summer and ginger lilies (*Hedychium*) and rosemary in autumn.

Contained Performers

Some plants are particularly suited to pot growth, growing naturally into attractive shapes without incessant upkeep and clipping. The newly released Boronia, *Boronia* 'Royale', grows naturally into a ball shape, and its blooms are deliciously perfumed for weeks on end during early spring.

Citrus make beautiful potted specimens and the fragrance of orange or lemon blossom is quite heady. Cumquats have aromatic foliage as well as scented blooms and tangy fruit. Mandarins, or tangerines (*Citrus reticulata)* are overlooked by many gardeners but

Pale Elegance

Cascading Wisteria fills the spring air with an exquisite perfume. Here the underplanting of Babiana highlights the lilac racemes. Some Wisteria cultivars take many years to flower and require full sun to flower well.

they are a versatile plant with delicious fruit, fragrant blooms and attractive foliage. Citrus tend to be shallow rooted so they should be kept moist.

For the classical garden, elegant pots and tubs filled with box, (*Buxus sempervirens*) provide a touch of formality. These slow-growing evergreen shrubs can be clipped into shapes and have a strangely spicy fragrance when trimmed. They can be cut into topiary, balls, spirals or standards shapes. Their rather insignificant flowers are usually clipped off when shaping.

Other fragrant plants suited to training into standards or domes include rosemary, lavender, bay and thyme.

Corsican mint (*Mentha requienii*) is also suited to containers, offering a lush cover that trails over the edges of pots and gives off a minty smell when lightly brushed.

Fragrant bulbs can also be used to great effect in containers, and when in flower, can be brought inside to brighten the home and replace cut flowers.

For healthy bulbs, use a good brand of potting mix and fertilise the plants as necessary with bulb food.

Native violet
(Viola hederacea)

Peace lily
(Spathiphyllum)

Shade tolerant

This window box is for windows without direct sunlight. The white peace lily flower will illuminate the shady aspect while the native violet will spill over with its delicate purple and white, softly scented flowers.

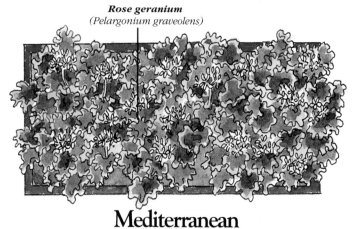

Rose geranium
(Pelargonium graveolens)

Mediterranean

The Mediterranean box reflects the European tradition of filling window boxes with Pelargoniums. This container is filled with the rose geranium, producing a cascade of scented leaves with soft pastel pink flowers.

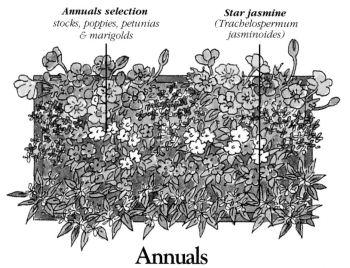

Annuals selection
stocks, poppies, petunias
& marigolds

Star jasmine
(Trachelospermum
jasminoides)

Annuals

By using annuals, this window box allows the viewer to enjoy the seasons. A selection of stocks, poppies, petunias and marigolds allows year-round colour and fragrance. The edges of this planter are softened by star jasmine which provides a beautiful heady scent in spring.

Window

*W*ho needs vast areas when all the colour, fragrance and beauty can be contained in mini gardens at our windowsills! Whether we have room for large gardens or not, there is something appealing about a fragrant window box. In Europe, towns or cities festooned with window boxes lend a cheerful welcoming air and it seems that even the drabbest of buildings can be revamped with a simple planting.

Window boxes bring colour and greenery to city dwellers, and the added dimension of fragrance makes them a great partner for the windowsill.

Frame a View

If you are in the inner city, plants can brighten a dreary outlook by framing a view or diverting the eye from a bad one. Window boxes certainly create a visual, cheery first impression. Filled with scented geraniums, night-scented stock, herbs such as thyme and pennyroyal, violets and jonquils, they can herald the change in seasons.

Aim to have a continuing display and include evergreens such as thyme, dwarf lavender, marjoram and sage among the bulbs and annuals. Perhaps

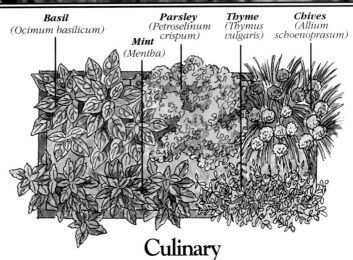

Culinary

A kitchen window box allows a cook quick access to an array of culinary herbs. A combination of basil, parsley, chives, mint and thyme provides the essential elements of many favourite dishes.

Labels: **Basil** (*Ocimum basilicum*), **Mint** (*Mentha*), **Parsley** (*Petroselinum crispum*), **Thyme** (*Thymus vulgaris*), **Chives** (*Allium schoenoprasum*)

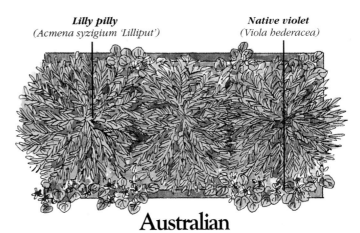

Australian

The Australian window box combines clipped lilly pilly 'Lilliput', which offers scented foliage along with the softly scented native violet to provide groundcover and spill from the container.

Labels: **Lilly pilly** (*Acmena syzigium 'Lilliput'*), **Native violet** (*Viola hederacea*)

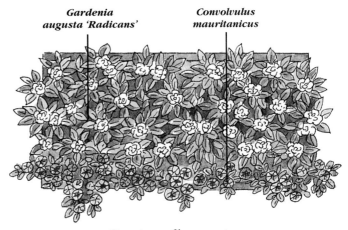

Spring flowering

The spring flowering window box combines the beautiful scent of the prostrate Gardenia with the delicate circular purple flowers of the Convolvulus. Its soft grey green foliage provides a great contrast with the dark glossy leaves of the Gardenia.

Labels: **Gardenia augusta 'Radicans'**, **Convolvulus mauritanicus**

Dressing

everyone in your household goes out to work or study during the day and only comes in late afternoon – try a night-scented planting scheme of white evening primrose, night-scented stock, white sand verbena, Abronia fragrans and sweet mignonette.

Choose compact plants that will not need constant cutting back to keep within bounds. Regular dead-heading will ensure continuous blooms and fortnightly applications of liquid fertiliser will keep plants healthy.

Water Well

Window boxes do dry out quickly, so keep them watered – at least every second day during warmer months. If you are going away for a weekend, fill an old narrow-necked drink bottle with water and up-end it into the soil. Tilt it slightly so that water seeps slowly into the soil. This is also an effective method with potted plants generally. Various products are available which can be added to potting mixes to enhance water holding.

Window boxes need not only be made of terracotta or stone. This charming and rustic wooden box, top, is filled with a mixture of culinary herbs, including chives.

Foliage can be just as fragrant as flowers. The placement of a selection of aromatic foliage plants through your garden will increase your enjoyment – leaves will release their fragrance when brushed past. The curry plant (*Helichysum italicum*) (1) with its aromatic silvery-grey foliage and yellow summer blooms makes a popular border plant. Zieria (2) is an Australian native shrub with four-petalled flowers and foliage with fragrance that is released when crushed. Lemon balm (*Melissa officinalis*) (3) is a sweetly scented herb with tangy foliage and white-pink summer flowers. Thyme (4) is great in paved areas as its fragrance is released when it is walked on.

Green Light

Rodney Hyett /Leigh Clapp /Don Brice

Using fragrant foliage in gardens

I t is possible to have a fragrant garden without a flower in sight as many plants have amazingly fragrant foliage, subtly scenting an entire garden or courtyard without a single bloom. Quite a different scent, it is far more piquant than that of flowers.

Plants suited to hot dry climates are often noted for their fragrant foliage - eucalypts, lavender and rosemary are among the most popular. To protect against water loss, these plants have developed a method of synthesizing essential oils, which are not as quick to evaporate as water.

Leaves actually hold their fragrance far longer than flowers. They are also sweeter when dried than when fresh. Planted along pathways, where you brush them as you walk along, or underfoot, so they are trodden on, will ensure that their scents are experienced.

Scented Geraniums

Scented-leafed geraniums (Pelargoniums) have quite inconspicuous flowers, but an amazing range of foliage offering scents such as nutmeg, cinnamon, lemon, orange, violet, almond and lavender. Large pots overflowing with these richly perfumed plants, with their sprinkling of tiny pink, lavender and white flowers, are ideal for planting on either side of doorways, gates or entrances.

There are at least 20 varieties of rose-scented geraniums, the strongest rose scent from the *P. capitatum* with its deep Attar of Roses fragrance. The lemon-scented geraniums include the citronella-scented *P. limoneum*, reputed to repel mosquitoes, while *P. crispum* has the aroma of freshly squeezed lemons.

Pelargoniums are popular – they are showy and remarkably hardy. Scented-leafed Pelargoniums (1) have small star-shaped flowers and are grown primarily for their fragrant foliage. Try a brilliant display of zonal Pelargoniums (2) with their showy blooms, or nutmeg-scented Pelargonium (3), with its mass of flowers among aromatic leaves.

Hyssopus, above left, has been grown since Biblical times for its healing powers as well as its aroma. It can be propagated from cuttings and is suitable to grow as a hedge. In summer its handsome spikes of blue flowers attract butterflies and bees.
The long-leafed wax flower (*Eriostemon myoporoides*), above right, has scented dark green leaves and white star-shaped flowers borne in clusters in spring. It makes a handsome medium to large compact evergreen shrub suited to hedging or screening.

The Essence of Herbs

Herbs are among the most popular of the scented foliage plants offering the tangy scent of lemon balm, the acrid scent of tansy and the sweet fragrance of eau-de-cologne mint. There are many types of thyme which can be used to wonderful effect as a border for garden beds, in cracks in paving, for edging paths, when overhanging stone retaining walls, and in tubs and pots.

Basil has a pungent spicy aroma; lemon verbena is citric and fresh, rosemary is pine-like, pennyroyal is distinctly pepperminty (and is also used as a mosquito repellant) and Balm of Gilead (*Cedronella canariensis*) is likened to the musty aroma of an antique bookshop!

Many Australian plants are noted far more for their fragrant foliage than their flowers. How often have you walked past a eucalypt tree and picked a leaf to crush, then breathed in the strong, fresh fragrance that so vividly recalls childhood walks in the bush or through a forest? The mint bushes, the eucalypts, tea trees, Croweas, Phebaliums, zierias and wax plants certainly refute the claim that Australian plants have no fragrance.

A Selection of Fragrant Foliage Plants

■ WILLOW MYRTLE (*Agonis flexuosa*): evergreen weeping tree with aromatic foliage and small white flowers in spring and summer. Grows to 10m (32ft).

■ BOTTLEBRUSH (*Callistemon citrinus*): Australian native shrubs with lemon-scented leaves and crimson flowers. Grows to 1.8m (6ft).

■ DARWINIA (*Darwinia citriodora*): Australian native low spreading shrub with lemon-scented leaves and reddish flowers in summer. Grows to 60cm (2ft).

■ DIOSMA (*Coleonema album*): evergreen heath-like shrub with highly aromatic lemon-green leaves and fragrant white single flowers in winter-spring. Grows to 1m (3ft).

■ WAXFLOWER (*Eriostemon myoporoides*): evergreen woody shrubs with aromatic foliage and single star-shaped flowers. Grows to 1m (3ft).

■ MYRTLE (*Myrtus communis*): evergreen shrub with aromatic foliage, scented flowers and dark autumn berries. Grows to 4m (13ft).

Making a Splash

Fragrant plants to grow in water environments

Rodney Hyett

Trisha Dixon

Waterlilies are the most exotic of all water plants and will flower in cool climate gardens as well as the tropics. Make sure your pool is not in complete shade or the blooms may never appear.

Water adds an entirely new dimension to a garden by adding a cool calming mood using sight and sound as inspiration. What better way to romanticise your garden than complementing a water garden with fragrant plants. However, much of the allure of water is in the reflections, so make sure that whatever plants you put in or around it do not take over! Colours can also appear different and create dramatic effects in water (eg. white blooms on or over water give the impression of reflected light).

Consider the growth habits of plants as the shade they create will increase as they grow. Also take into account the surface area and depth of a pond; it should be 45-60cm (18in-2ft) deep as water plants need a consistent temperature to achieve maximum growth. The more sun that reaches water, the wider the choice of plants which can be grown, as plants such as waterlilies demand full sun.

Waterlilies are not only beautiful, but many have the added allure of being fragrant as well.

Nymphaea odorata 'Alba' is a hardy white lily requiring water 40cm (16in) in depth.

N. odorata 'Minor' is a particularly fragrant white waterlily and only needs 15cm–25cm (6in-10in) water.

N. tuberosa 'Rosea' has shell pink flowers and needs water 30cm–45cm (12in-18in) in depth.

When considering placing waterlilies in a pond make sure that no more than one-third of the surface area of the water is taken up with the plants and remember that each waterlily requires one square metre of water over which to spread.

Much of the beauty of water in the garden is in the surrounding landscape and many plants enjoy the slightly damp conditions this provides. One such plant is the vanilla lily (*Sowerbaea juncea*), an Australian native with small pink-violet spring blooms with a vanilla fragrance. Plant in full sun and keep moist.

The common primrose (*Primula vulgaris*), enjoys the moist areas around a pond and has delicately sweet yellow flowers during spring. This is a hardy perennial that grows to 15cm (6in) in height.

TERRACED GARDEN

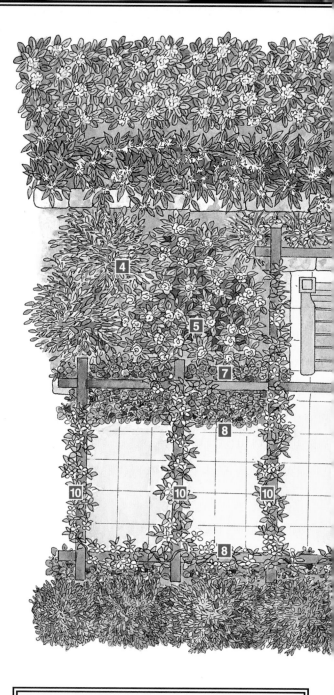

This fragrant terraced garden with scented pergola has been designed for gardens with a steep gradient. Much of the natural gradient found in gardens is sloping and difficult to work with. However, the terraced garden provides an opportunity to retain sloping areas into smaller spaces providing room for level areas, such as pathways and open lawns. It also allows space for plant specimens to be viewed.

In this terraced garden, a manicured fragrant hedge is used to screen the boundary fence. Below the orange jessamine is a low mound hedge of Trachelospermum which spills over the top wall, softening its structure and providing a beautiful scent in spring. The garden bench is surrounded by Gardenias with their glossy green leaves and wonderfully perfumed white flowers, and French lavender, *Lavandula dentata*, with its soft grey, pungent foliage.

Behind the bench, wild Iris provides a linear pattern, its leaves punctuated with delicate white and purple flowers. Spilling over the lower wall is Convolvulus a groundcover with small circular purple flowers, which close at night, and soft grey-green foliage.

Sweet violets edge both sides of the path, while a low clipped box hedge traces the pathway. A scented pergola produces an array of scents for the visitor to enjoy. Climbers such as Clematis, honeysuckle and Carolina jasmine provide shade and a romantic feel to the garden.

Key for Plan

1. **Orange jessamine** *(Murraya paniculata)*
2. **Trachelospermum asiaticum**
3. **Wild Iris** *(Dietes vegeta)*
4. **French lavender** *(Lavandula dentata)*
5. **Gardenia augusta**
6. **Honeysuckle** *(Lonicera species)*
7. **Convolvulus** *(Convolvulus sabatius)*
8. **Sweet violet** *(Viola odorata)*
9. **Carolina jasmine** *(Gelsemium sempervirens)*
10. **Clematis montana**
11. **Box** *(Buxus sempervirens)*

A terraced fragrant garden is pretty and practical for a garden with a steep gradient.

Rubiaceae - The Gardenia family

This family originates in the more tropical parts of the world and gives us some of the most exquisitely fragrant flowers that nature has to offer. They tend to have glossy green leaves and snow white blossoms.

Bouvardia longiflora:
A frost tender, evergreen shrub with highly fragrant, white, tubular flowers.

❖

Coffea arabica:
Commonly known as the coffee tree. As well as producing coffee beans it has fragrant white flowers.

❖

Gardenia augusta:
The common Gardenia, it is a compact shrub with single white flowers. Wonderful short-term cut flowers.

❖

Gardenia augusta 'Radians':
A low growing form of the common Gardenia with smaller flowers. Excellent as a groundcover.

❖

Gardenia augusta 'Magnifica':
A double-flowered shrub form.

❖

Randia species:
Beautiful white-flowered shrub similar in appearance to Gardenia.

❖

Rothmannia globosa:
Commonly known as the tree Gardenia, it is a small tree with masses of white flowers in spring.

❖

Wallflowers (*Cheiranthus cheiri*) thrive in the sun.

Mock orange (*Philadelphus*) tolerates full sun.

Boronia flowers in sun, but keep roots cool by mulching.

Rodney Hyett/Dale Harvey

Sun & Shade Plants

Sun-loving Plants

As a rule, most fragrant perennials and annuals need full sun to flower. Shrubs such as mock orange, lilac, roses, rosemary, Buddleia, Cistus, Daphne, Deutzia, Prostanthera, Boronia, Bouvardia, Brunsfelsia, Choisya, Gardenia and Viburnums will also flower best in full sun. Most of these plants, will however, appreciate protection from hot afternoon sun in summer.

One of the most obligingly fragrant perennials for full sun conditions is the wallflower (*Cheiranthus cheiri*). Remarkably hardy and tenacious, it will grow in the most impossible positions, in crevices of walls or steps. Its only requisite is full sun to flower. Colours range from orange and yellow to mauve and pink. Growing to 90cm (3ft) in height, they are very free flowering. To prevent plants becoming lanky, cut back the stems after flowering.

Rewarding Lupins

Another perennial demanding full sun to flower is the lupin with its dense spikes of pea flowers. Not all are scented, but those that have a strong fragrance include *Lupinus arboreus*, *L. densiflorus* and *L. luteus*. Lupins are rewarding to grow because of their long flowering season throughout summer. They are hardy, easy to grow and come in a range of colours from blue, white, pink and yellow and all shades in between!

All of the herbs thrive in full sun, so even if you haven't the inclination for a herb garden, don't overlook lavender, bergamot, rosemary or basil. They need no special attention other than an annual prune and will fill the garden with perfume and colour for months on end.

Lily of the valley favours a shady spot.

Magnolia soulangeana 'Lennei' prefers filtered light.

Shade-loving Plants

O smanthus is a genus of evergreen shrubs with memorable fragrance that is suited to growing in filtered sunlight. It is a wonderful choice for a hedge or planting under the eaves of a house so that the scent can be carried through open windows and doors.

Eucryphia is another genus of shrubs grown for fragrant flowers and attractive foliage. They grow best with roots in a cool, moist shaded position in soil with neutral to acidic pH. *Eucryphia glutinosa* bears large fragrant white flowers throughout summer and the glossy dark green leaves turn orange-red in autumn. Deciduous, they grow to 10m (30ft). Leatherwood (*Eucryphia lucida*) has smaller single rose-like white blooms throughout summer on a more upright evergreen tree. Grows to 10m (30ft).

Many Magnolias including *Magnolia x soulangeana* and *M. liliflora* 'Nigra' enjoy the protection of filtered sunlight. The heady fragrance of the port wine Magnolia (*Michelia figo*) is really treasured, as are its exquisite blooms in spring. To ensure best results, add peat or leaf-mould when planting and keep the water up in the first few years.

Glorious Perfumes

Daphne is synonymous with winter fragrance, but there is a price to pay for such a glorious, heady perfume. Daphne does need coddling. It needs precisely the right position and doesn't take kindly to being neglected. Afternoon shade is a must, so a sheltered, east-facing position is ideal. Keep the plants well protected from the hot summer sun and don't allow it to dry out in summer. Daphne is not at all partial to lime, so mulch with well-rotted horse or cow manure and plenty of compost.

A fragrant groundcover for shady areas is lily of the valley, with its haunting fragrance, so rarely emulated in perfumes, soaps and powders. Once established, it will spread readily, providing a fragrant carpet throughout spring. Plant pips (bulb-like structures that the plant forms) in a sheltered position with morning sun. Add leaf mould, lawn clippings and well-rotted animal manure to enrich the soil. Not suited to tropical climes, lily of the valley favours cool conditions.

Cover Up

Fragrant climbing plants

C limbers are among the most romantic of all plants. Wisteria, Clematis, sweet peas and rambling roses are just a few of the plants that can be used to clothe walls, camouflage buildings, drape over arches and festoon fences. Honeysuckle, jasmine, Gelsemium, Stephanotis, Trachelospermum and Mandevilla make the palette even more extensive to draw on when choosing fragrant climbers.

The true jasmines are the epitome of fragrance, and there are so many to choose from that it is possible to have a jasmine in flower every season of the year. They are more at home in the tropics, but will survive in sheltered corners in cooler gardens. *Jasminum officinale* and the larger flowered *J. rex* provide fragrance throughout summer and *J. azoricum* blooms throughout autumn into winter. The primrose jasmine, *J. mesneyi* heralds spring with its soft primrose blooms and *J. polyanthum* flourishes in the warmer weather, providing a bounteous supply of blooms and fragrance for an all too brief period in spring. However, beware of planting it in courtyards, this jasmine can be rather overpowering in enclosed areas.

Tropical Climbers

Tropical gardens seem to be a haven of fragrant plants and there are a number of scented climbers available. These include the *Beaumontia grandiflora*, a woody vine with fragrant clusters of creamy-white bells; Madagascar jasmine (*Stephanotis floribunda*) with its beautiful waxy clusters of fragrant flowers and glossy green leaves and Chilean jasmine (*Mandevilla suaveolens*) with its Gardenia-scented white trumpet flowers.

More suited to the cooler climes are the various species of *Clematis*. The evergreen *Clematis armandii* is the most obliging with its vanilla-scented waxy cream flowers. This is a handsome climber with dark green leaves and vigorous growth. The simple single white *Clematis montana* also has a subtle sweet vanilla fragrance; it is more noticeable when planted in an enclosed area such as a courtyard. The Australian native Clematis,

Simon Kenny/Dale Harvey/Rodney Hyett

The beauty of Wisteria in full bloom is a sight to behold. This old-fashioned flowering climber is laden with richly scented blooms in late spring, and is an elegant choice for either a sprawling country garden or a smart townhouse pergola.

Honey-sweet honeysuckle is a quick growing climber.

Sweet peas will bloom for months on end.

The snail creeper (*Phaseolus caracalla*) is an evergreen.

Leigh Clapp/Brent Wilson/Dale Harvey/Rodney Hyett, (Eastcott Nursery, far left)

Brightly coloured stocks and sweet peas bloom against a backdrop formed by an entire wall of cat's claw creeper (1). A mauve Wisteria adds to the fragrance.

Pink jasmine (*Jasminum polyanthum*) (2) and white broom (*Cytisus*) provide abundant blooms and heady perfume in this early spring scene.

The pink blooms of this honeysuckle (*Lonicera korolkowii*) (3) provide an effective background to the perennial border in front. With its exceptional fragrance, it makes a delightful cover-up plant; if you want a fence or wall covered in a hurry, honeysuckle will do the job. Ensure it has some shade.

Although the name is a something of a mouthful, 'Souvenir de Madam Leonie Viennot' (4) is a beautifully scented, repeat flowering, climbing tea rose. Here, it clambers over a white picket fence, the apricot blush blooms complemented by its lush, shiny green foliage.

Clematis aristata is also sweetly scented and is aptly named travellers' joy. In spring its small star-shaped flowers are followed by fluffy white seed heads. The subtle light green blooms of *C. parviflora* have a charming and distinct lemon fragrance.

Sweet Poison

Daturas (*syn Brugmansia*) call attention to themselves, not only for their unusual trumpet like flowers but for their overpowering perfume, particularly in the evenings. Little wonder they have been labelled angels' trumpets. However, beware all that is sweet – Daturas are deadly poisonous – both flowers and seeds. *Datura candida* is one of the most elegant of flowers with its sweetly scented white trumpets on show from summer to autumn. *D. suaveolens* has double white fragrant blooms in autumn and winter, while *D. cornigera* has pointed semi-double flowers. For coloured trumpets, try *D. meteloides* for mauve trumpets and *D. chlorantha* for its trumpet-shaped yellow flowers.

66

Clematis have the most subtle of fragrances and this *Clematis montana* is one of the most popular of spring climbers with its simple star-shaped blooms.

Irises can have the most enticing of fragrances but as not all are scented, select Iris when in flower and do the "sniff test". This German bearded Iris, right, adds a sweet fragrance and contrasts well with the blue Cynoglossum.

It is surprising that such intense fragrance can be emitted by such small blooms as these hyacinths (1). They will flower for years as long as they are watered and fertilised after flowering as this is when bulbs store energy for the following year's flowering.

The Japanese Iris (*Iris kaempferi*) (2) looks wonderful when planted in bold sweeps but it has only the slightest fragrance unlike the old flag or bearded Iris.

Jonquils (3) are richly scented bulbs that begin flowering in late autumn and continue until early spring.

The delicate looking lily of the valley (*Convallaria majalis*) (4) requires cool woodland conditions with rich soil and semi-shade to flourish and spread rapidly.

Beautiful Bulbs

Dale Harvey/Rodney Hyett

Scented treasures in little packages

Think of fragrant bulbs and lily of the valley will immediately spring to mind, along with lilies, jonquils, freesias and tuberose. Don't disregard the Iris – some are evocatively scented while others have no scent whatsoever. Day lilies, particularly *Hemerocallis fragrans* are beautifully fragrant as are the spider lilies (*Hymenocallis*) and the rather stiff hyacinths are noted for their perfume; some orchids are also blessed with scent.

Lovely Lilies

Lilies have an enticing fragrance that make them wonderful in the garden or for elegant flower arrangements. Not all are fragrant, but the most overwhelming is the madonna lily (*Lilium candidum*) with its pure white languid blooms – so elegant and regal and yet so generous in fragrance. The Christmas or Easter lily (*Lilium longiflorum*) is not quite as exotic but so stately in the garden. The oriental lilies (*Lilium auratum*) are treasured for their coloured blooms in pink, white or cream.

The exquisitely fragrant tuberose, (*Polianthes tuberosa*)

Creamy Freesias

The old-fashioned cream freesias, (*Freesia refracta*) have a special fragrance all of their own and are remarkably easy to grow. Steer away from the brightly coloured hybrids which have little in the way of scent to recommend them, the pale yellow and creamy white ones are the true scented varieties. A wonderful bulb to naturalise under trees, they can be planted in autumn – make sure they are protected from the hot afternoon sun. These spring-flowering bulbs actually belong to the Iris family and are native to South Africa.

is a favourite of florists for bridal bouquets. An autumn-flowering bulb, it will actually flower throughout the year in mild climates, requiring only to be planted in a sheltered site in full sun.

Among the most exotic of the fragrant bulbs are the ginger lilies, particularly the white ginger lily (*Hedychium coronarium*) with its delicate butterfly-like, intensely fragrant white blooms. The Kahili ginger (*H. gardnerianum*) is also exotically fragrant with orchid-like golden blooms. Ginger lilies have been described as amongst the most sweetly perfumed of all flowers.

Narcissus

A bunch of the old double jonquils is enough to scent an entire room. Not all *Narcissus* (which includes daffodils and jonquils) are as scented as the jonquils, but try 'Erlicheer', 'Paper Whites' or 'Yellow Cheerfulness' to grow in the far corners of your garden or, if space is limited, grow them in pots. Order bulbs late summer and plant early autumn for early spring flowering.

Hedge Rows

Fragrant enclosures and screens

Rosemary, lavender, mint bush and honeysuckle are some of the plants that are perfectly suited to creating hedges, either clipped every few months or allowed to grow naturally. Or try a tapestry hedge of fragrant plants that perform at different times of year: a Viburnum base for winter flowers, Wisteria for spring, a summer flowering rose such as *Rosa filipes* 'Kiftsgate' and a Virginia creeper (*Parthenocissus quinquefolia*) for brilliant autumn foliage.

Roses such as 'Stanwell Perpetual' and the rugosas such as 'Blanc Double de Coubert' and *Rosa rugosa* 'Alba' make stunning fragrant hedges with their scented blooms. They are all continuous flowering roses with coloured heps that are decorative in autumn and winter. The Scotch Burnett roses, such as *Rosa andrewsii,* are well suited to informal hedging and have superb autumn foliage.

Versatile and Different

Viburnums are among the most versatile and handsome shrubs for taller hedges, and yet are rarely used. They offer variety, too, as there are 120 species from which to choose. *Viburnum x carlcephalum* bears large rounded heads of fragrant white flowers throughout spring on a rounded, bushy, vigorous growing shrub to 2m (6ft). *Viburnum carlesii* is a shrub for all seasons with fragrant flowers in spring, followed by decorative black fruit and autumn tonings well into winter. *V. x burkwoodii* is the most beautifully perfumed.

Rhododendrons are not commonly recognised for their fragrance yet there are a number of tropical (vireya) rhododendrons that have quite a distinctive perfume, and they make superb hedges. If you like rhododendrons, keep an eye out for *R. konori, R. herzogii, R. loranthiflorum, R. gardenia* and 'Highland Arabesque'.

Warm Weather Friends

Plants that are suitable for tall evergreen hedges to 3m (10ft) in warm climate gardens include the orange jessamine (*Murraya paniculata)* with its orange blossom-scented blooms in spring and summer; the port wine magnolia (*Michelia figo*) with its deliciously scented creamy yellow blooms throughout spring and summer and very handsome glossy green foliage year-round; *Carpenteria californica* is a crowd-stopper with its fragrant pure white single blooms and yellow stamens with glossy green foliage; and the lemon-scented tea-tree (*Leptospermum petersonii*) is a fast-growing Australian native with small, white, five-petalled flowers in spring and early summer.

A stunning taller screening plant suited to enclosing boundaries or providing privacy from neighbours is *Michelia doltsopa* which flowers profusely throughout winter and spring with the most sweetly scented blooms of lush creamy white. This evergreen tree has glossy, dark green leaves and grows to 10m (30ft); it prefers a sunny, sheltered position in a frost-free garden.

Creating a Hedge

To create a formal hedge you should plant the hedging shrubs closer together than you would in the normal garden, allow for an intermingling of branches. Generally, plant about 1m (3ft) apart and begin tip-pruning immediately to create bushy plants.

Tip-pruning means regularly pinching out the shoot tips during the growing season. This type of regular pruning will avoid the hedge becoming leggy and sparse. If you let the plants grow to their desired height first, you will never shape them properly nor will they be evenly dense.

If you are after a quick growing, aromatic hedge, Buddleias fit the bill. *Buddleia salvifolia* has honey-scented blooms in late winter and early spring with fine grey-green leaves on a dense evergreen shrub.

Clipped rosemary, top, makes a handsome hedge suited to both large formal gardens or small cottage gardens. French lavender (*Lavandula dentata*), left, makes an attractive hedge year-round with its plump mauve flowers and soft grey foliage.

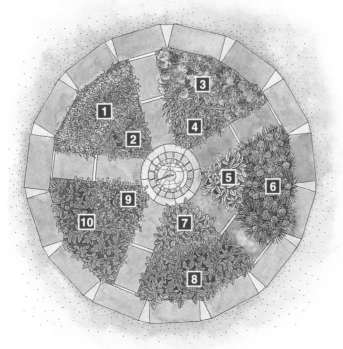

Dale Harvey

A Traditional Herb Wheel

An old-fashioned way to enjoy aromatic herbs is to plant them in a circle approximately 2m (6ft) in diameter and set rows of bricks fanning out from the centre to the rim. This idea is derived from the old custom of using abandoned cartwheels as kitchen herb garden "planners". It is a really useful device where space is limited, such as in a small courtyard garden.

Ideally, it should be located close to the kitchen door as it provides many of the most commonly used kitchen herbs. This particular design uses the traditional edging to define the circular pattern and dividers. There is a variety of ground-covering herbs such as parsley, thyme, mint, basil and chives, which are allowed to spill over the brick edging.

A herb wheel is also an ideal way of containing the often vigorous growth of mints. Try planting a mixture, such as apple mint, peppermint, spearmint and pennyroyal with bergamot to create a clean refreshing bouquet of scents that will appeal to bees and humans alike. Towards the centre, larger herbs such as tarragon, sage, lemon balm and coriander can encircle a focal point such as this sundial set on a plinth.

Key for Plan

1	**Thyme** (*Thymus vulgaris*)	**6**	**Chives** (*Allium schoenoprasum*)
2	**Basil** (*Ocimum basilicum*)	**7**	**Lemon balm** (*Melissa officinalis*)
3	**Parsley** (*Petroselinum crispum*)	**8**	**Basil** (*Ocimum basilicum*)
4	**Tarragon** (*Artemisia dracunculus*)	**9**	**Coriander** (*Coriandrum sativum*)
5	**Sage** (*Salvia officinalis*)	**10**	**Mint** (*Mentha piperita*)

Perfumed Paths

Even the smallest path can be canopied with perfumed climbing plants and edged with low-growing plants that release scent as they are brushed against as above.

If you are making a path with pavers or old bricks, leave 5cm (2in) square gaps randomly and plant them with aromatic herbs of a carpeting habit. Allow the path to meander – even in a tiny garden this will create a greater impression of space.

Some of the most ideal aromatic herbs to plant by and in your path are thyme and mint. Mint is exceptionally hardy. Among the best choices for thyme are the prostrate thymes, especially Thymus serpyllum, or Mother of Thyme (Thymus praecox). You might also like to mass clusters of the different types of pinks, mints (eg. apple mint, spearmint, peppermint) along the sides of a path.

Other dwarfish plants to set alongside a path include rosemary and, in the sunniest spots, a fairy miniature rose, which adds colour, if not fragrance. It is also hard to beat lavender for rich scent and colour.

You could also set potted scented Pelargoniums up the sides of a path or stone stairs, a fashion which started in Victorian times, when the wide crinolines would brush the leaves, releasing the spicy fragrance. Perhaps the favourite pelargonium is Pelargonium capitatum, now cultivated for its essence, which replaces rose attar in many perfumes. However, if you like spicy aromas, the lemony P. crispum varieties will suit. Other scented plants that are particularly suited to bringing fragrance to pathways are hyacinths, stocks and wallflowers.

Scent-sational Ideas

Rodney Hyett

Aromatic Arches

An arch may be rounded or square, made of woven twigs, wood, or even sturdy, maintenance free metal or plastic.

The dainty, primrose-like flowers of *Jasminum officinale* are a fitting choice. Set rosemary or lavender bushes at the base and perhaps train a tobacco plant (*Nicotiana alata*) up the other side.

Every romantic arch should have at least one of the honeysuckles growing upon it. *Lonicera periclymenum* blooms in high summer. Perhaps the loveliest of all is *L. japonica*, with its sweetly-scented creamy yellow flowers; there's also the giant honeysuckle (*Lonicera hildebrandiana*). *Clematis vitalba* is another lovely choice, with its clusters of greeny-white flowers.

Climbing scented roses, of course, need little introduction. For a scented arch, or for training along a wooden fence or a brick wall, the rich sweet scent of the pink rambler rose 'Albertine' is hard to beat.

Scented Seats

Take a rest in your garden and enjoy the fragrance. Try growing lavender, right, through a wooden bench. You could also build a simple bench against a brick wall or the side of the house, by making a 'trough' from bricks or railway sleepers and filling it with soil before planting thickly with a scented groundcover, such as thyme or pennyroyal.

by Pamela Allardice

Cottage Charm

Fragrance in a Cottage Garden

The appealing yet unkempt style of cottage gardens, with their masses of different flowering and foliage plants, can be complemented by the delicate scents of fragrant plants. The hallmark of a cottage garden is informality – every piece of ground is used. Trailing blooms and small, pastel-coloured flowers have added depth when their sweet scents come wafting through the carefully designed disorder.

Fragrance is often a feature of the most commonly favoured cottage garden plants. A mixture of scented flowers and herbs can add interest to the charming chaos of the garden.

Pure Fragrance

The mock oranges are almost unrivalled with their rich fragrance, innocence of form and hardiness. Their scent is indescribably sweet. *Philadelphus coronarius* with its four-petalled flowers; *P.* 'Belle Etoile' with its violet centres and *P.* 'Virginal' with its double flowers are special favourites.

Cheddar pinks such as this *Dianthus gratianopolitanus* (1) are old favourites of the cottage garden with their sweet fragrance and mound of evergreen grey foliage. Sweet peas (2), a signature plant of this garden style, will provide fragrance through the winter. Mock orange, *Philadelphus* (3), is a mainstay of the cottage garden with its superbly fragrant, pure white spring blooms; it grows readily from cuttings.

Simon Kenny (Garden of Gledswood Homestead, NSW, right)/ Dale Harvey

A sundial makes a perfect centrepiece, surrounded by heartsease (*Viola tricolor*), catmint and lavender.

Pinks (*Dianthus*) are also synonymous with the cottage garden. Affectionately known as gilliflowers, they are overwhelmingly fragrant, reminiscent of spicy cloves, vanilla and spice and all things nice. Pinks are a type of low growing carnation and are easily struck from cuttings making it a breeze to line pathways with clumps of them, and sending up a myriad of flowers to scent the air. Favourites include 'Mrs Sinkins' and 'Old English Mauve'.

The flag Iris can be a hardy mainstay of any old-fashioned garden. The old flag Iris have the most evocative scent – quite irresistible once encountered. Just one or two blooms of the white *Iris albicans* in a vase can scent an entire room. The wonderful thing about Iris is that once you have a small rhizome (a creeping underground stem), you can keep dividing until you have dozens of Iris. They are also incredibly tough, needing little attention throughout the year other than a handful of fertiliser at the end of winter.

Sweet peas (*Lathyrus odoratus*) are a signature plant of the cottage garden. Seek out the old-fashioned varieties as they are far more scented than the modern, more freely flowering types; lavender and blue blooms are said to the most sweetly scented. Sow seeds in their final position, as they are hard to transplant and provide a support such as a trellis. Remove spent flowers to encourage further blooms and add lime to acidic soils and blood and bone when preparing for planting.

Leigh Clapp (Garden at Red Cow Farm, NSW)

Leigh Clapp (Red Cow Farm, NSW)

This is a classic cottage garden, left, complete with a picket fence enclosing a small space filled to overflowing with roses such as the pink 'Mary Rose' and the white 'Lamarque' trailing along the verandah. The rambling feeling of the garden is enhanced with the choice of other special cottage favourites, such as catmint, delphiniums and even garlic, a natural way to keep the aphids at bay!

The warmth and protection of this high stone wall, above, provides a great backdrop for this pure cottage garden of aquilegias, poppies, golden mock orange, delphiniums, *Alchemilla mollis*, foxgloves, catmint, Clematis and two fragrant roses – 'Paul's Lemon Pillar' cascading over the wall and the pink blooms of 'Blarii No.2' scrambling up to meet it.

Scents 'that hang in the air':

'An edging of Cheddar pinks. A hedge of hybrid musk roses, especially 'Penelope'. Some bushes of the rugosa rose, 'Blanc double de Coubert'. Azaleas. A hedge of sweetbriar. The balsam poplar when it first unfolds its sticky leaves. Lilium auratum, as a luxury. Humea elegans, the incense plant, another luxury because it has to be raised in heat and planted out for the summer.'

– Vita Sackville-West

Lavandula stoechas

Lavandula viridis

Lavandula dentata

Lavandula dentata 'Allardii'

Sweet, Sweet LAVENDER

Lavender is another mainstay of the cottage garden with its distinctive mauve and highly fragrant blooms throughout summer. Lavender walkways, tubs of lavender, clipped hedges around the herb garden and borders for the flower garden – there can never be too much lavender in a cottage garden. Lavender has Mediterranean origins and is incredibly hardy. It thrives in dry gardens, only requiring plenty of sun to flower, slightly alkaline soil and good drainage. Always cut back after flowering to prevent the plant becoming too woody.

Pick of the Bunch

Lavandula angustifolia, English lavender, is highly fragrant and suited to borders and hedges. The semi-dwarf 'Hidcote' makes a wonderful low clipped hedge.

Lavandula angustifolia 'Alba', white lavender, is an upright highly fragrant pure white form of English lavender, suited to hedging. The miniature white lavender, 'Dwarf White', is wonderful for edging paths.

Lavandula angustifolia 'Hidcote Pink', pink lavender, is a form of English lavender not quite as floriferous as the mauve lavenders but it has distinctive pink blooms.

Lavandula dentata, French Lavender, has soft lavender-blue flowers throughout the year. Lavandula dentata 'Allardii is the largest growing lavender, reaching more than 1.3m (4ft) in height.

Lavandula stoechas, Italian lavender, has deep purple blooms and self seeds readily. Lavandula stoechas 'Pendunculata' has exceptionally long bracts.

Lavandula viridis, green lavender, has curious yellow-green fragrant blooms on a sprawling low shrub.

French Lavender (*Lavandula dentata*) is the most obliging of all lavenders and it is well-suited to dry gardens.

Simon Kenny (Garden of Gledswood Homestead, NSW, left)/Rodney Hyett

Scented Gifts from Your

Gentle Flower Balm

Use this freshening lotion to whisk away the last traces of makeup, soap and grime which can dull the skin. Store in a cool dark place and use within 2 months.

2 tablespoons strong
    chamomile tea
2 tablespoons strong
    elderflower tea
50ml rosewater
2 teaspoons witch-hazel
1 teaspoon glycerine

Pour all ingredients into a dark-coloured glass bottle, seal. Shake well before applying with a cotton ball.

Bedknob Sachets

1 cup hops
1/2 cup fresh mint leaves
1/2 cup sweet woodruff
1/2 cup fresh lavender petals
1 tablespoon southernwood
50cm muslin or cotton, cut into
    10cm squares
string or ribbon, for tying

Crush herbs slightly, mix together in a china bowl. Spoon mixture into centre of muslin, tie securely with string. Stitch on string or ribbon loops, hang on bedpost or over a lampshade where the scent will permeate the room.

Scented Washballs

75g soft unscented soap, grated
125ml rosewater
rose or geranium essential oil
1 tablespoon each dried rose
    petals, marjoram, and lavender,
    processed to a fine powder
vegetable colouring, if desired

Melt soap in small saucepan over a low heat. Combine with rosewater, stirring thoroughly. Cool slightly. Add essential oil, powdered herbs and colouring; mix well. Roll mixture into small balls. Stand balls on a piece of waxed paper in the sun for about 2 hours. Wet your hands with a little extra rosewater and polish each ball until smooth. Allow to dry completely. Store in a jar in a cool, dry place.

Flower Sugar

Be sure to use edible flower petals that have not been sprayed with an insecticide or a pesticide.
Substitute scented flower sugar for ordinary sugar when preparing puddings or creamy desserts, or add it to whipped cream or custards.

Combine caster (superfine) sugar with a handful of scented petals (fragrant roses, violets, lavender, honeysuckle or clove pinks are suitable) in a canister. Seal.

Scented Bath Bag

3 teaspoons lemon balm
1 teaspoon fresh rosemary
1 teaspoon fresh chamomile
    flowers
2 teaspoons bran
new small towelling face cloth

Place all the ingredients in the centre of the cloth. Secure firmly with ribbon. Before getting in the bath, wet the bag and squeeze it to release the milky bran and scented essences. Use the bag to scrub yourself gently all over and perfume the skin.

Sunshine Potpourri

2 tablespoons southernwood
2 tablespoons marigold flowers
1 tablespoon tansy buttons
1 tablespoon yellow everlasting
    daisies
2 tablespoons fresh lemon thyme
1 tablespoon nutmeg chips
1 tablespoon fresh bay leaves
2 tablespoons orris root powder
lemon essential oil

Combine dry ingredients in a large china or pottery dish; add 6-10 drops essential oil, mix together. Display in a decorative bowl.

Lavender Wands

A favourite gift is the scented lavender wand or bottle. You will need about 75 lavender heads to make 5 wands.

lavender heads with stems at least
    15cm long
string or ribbon

Take a bunch of 15 lavender heads. Using a piece of string about 1m long, tie the bunch together with string under flower heads, wind string around flower heads, tie to secure. Bend the stems back gently below the string so they form a cage

Garden

over the flowers, making sure the stems are evenly spaced. Tie the stems together with string at top of flower heads. Trim ends of stems so they are even. If using ribbon, a pretty effect can be achieved by weaving the long end of ribbon over and under the stems, moving down until all the lavender is enclosed. Stitch the ribbon ends securely together, and finish with a bow. Dry wands out of direct sunlight.

Crystallised Mint Leaves

20-30 fresh mint leaves
2 egg whites, lightly whisked
small pastry brush
1/2 cup (110g) caster sugar

Preheat oven to 120°C. Gently rinse mint leaves, pat dry with absorbent paper to remove all moisture; leaves must be dry. Brush leaves very lightly all over with egg white. Sprinkle lightly with caster sugar. Place on greaseproof paper. Bake for 8-10 minutes, or until leaves are crisp.

Scented Teas

Be sure to use flower petals and herbs that have not been sprayed with an insecticide or a pesticide.

Scented flower teas are calming and refreshing, as they do not contain caffeine. In summer, chill scented flower tea and add a little honey for a delicious iced drink. Do not forget that picking the flowers for your teapot is itself a relaxing pastime. Try the following combinations:

❖ *lavender and chamomile*

❖ *rose petal and chamomile*

❖ *lavender and rosemary flower*

❖ *lime flower and mint leaves*

Fragrant Fan

Decorate a straw fan with a posy of dried flowers, or a tiny sachet of potpourri tied on with a ribbon to ensure a fragrant breeze on a hot day.

These delightful fragrant gifts are the perfect tokens for birthdays, whenever visitors come to stay or, for pampering yourself. Bedknob Sachets, left, are a lovely welcoming touch for guests' bedrooms. Lavender Wands, above, can be tucked in among underwear or placed in the bathroom to add a sweet scent.

by Pamela Allardice

Create a herbal walk (1) by planting low growing herbs such as oregano and thyme in pockets along the paving.
A tapestry of colour in this potager garden with thyme, sage and oregano growing amongst the coloured leafed lettuce (2).
A herb garden (3), enclosed by a stone wall topped with a hedge of lavender, can be glimpsed through an open gate.
A pocket of herbs in a large garden - borage, marjoram, oregano and rosemary (4).

Herb Gardens

Rosemary

H erb beds create a scented garden within themselves as there are really no herbs devoid of any fragrance. Whether you have visions of an intricate formal herb garden or have room for only a few pots at the back door, these will be your most rewarding of plants for bloom, fragrance and usefulness. To be able to pick a bunch of mint to add to a summer drink, a sprig of rosemary to flavour a leg of lamb, or a handful of herbs for the salad bowl, is a delight since the herbs grown in your garden are infinitely more tasty than those that come from a jar.

There is something romantic about creating a herb garden and there is certainly no end to the possibilities in terms of design. Whether you choose to create a copy of a medieval apothecary's garden, simply plant thymes around a sundial, or

choose to grow a wild country herb garden, this design feature will be an added attraction to your entire garden scheme.

Start with a Plan

However small, a focal point can be the making of a herb garden. A bird bath, dovecote, simple piece of statuary, clipped standard bay tree or an urn overflowing with herbs can add an individual and romantic touch to your garden.

Before rushing off and planting lavender hedges, put some of your ideas down onto paper. It can be fun to try your hand at a number of different designs which can be finally transposed onto graph paper or drawn to scale on art paper. Allow enough room for paths, and be sure to take into account the sprawling habit of many herbs such as lavender, rosemary, sage and wormwood

Companion Planting

Companion planting means growing certain plants with others for their mutual benefit. For example, the roots of some plants are close to the surface while those of others penetrate deeply into the soil; these plants can be grown together because they are not competing for soil space. It is believed that the smell of certain herbs deters some insects from attacking plants, and reduces or eliminates the need for spraying.

Basil
Plant near tomatoes and asparagus.

Chamomile
Good companion to onions and cabbage.

Chives
Deters many insects – particularly good near carrots and apple trees.

Garlic
Deters aphids from roses, leaf curl on peach trees, insects in the orchard and kitchen garden.

Mint
Deters ants and helps cabbages and tomatoes.

Nasturtiums
Repel woolly aphids in apple trees.

Parsley
Good planted near roses, beans, chives and carrots.

Rosemary
Plant near beans, cabbages and carrots.

Unusual Herbs

Not unlike thyme is SAVORY of Crete (Satureia thymifolia), a small savory with tiny honey-scented pink flowers. The Costa Rica Mint Bush is another fragrant savory with a strong pennyroyal scent. The savories are among the most fragrant of herbs – particularly loved by bees.

ANISE is a small annual which produces licorice-flavoured seeds; it is used extensively in medicines and as flavouring in drinks and cooking. The plant has finely serrated leaves and small white flowers.

EYEBRIGHT is another small dainty annual with rather insignificant white flowers. Essentially a medicinal herb, as its name implies, it is used as a remedy for eye complaints! Eyebright tea is said to be a remedy for hayfever.

CUMIN is grown for its seed which is used in savoury dishes. The plant is a slender annual with small umbels of pink or white flowers. Grow from seed.

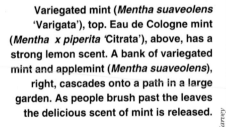

Variegated mint (*Mentha suaveolens* 'Varigata'), top. Eau de Cologne mint (*Mentha x piperita* 'Citrata'), above, has a strong lemon scent. A bank of variegated mint and applemint (*Mentha suaveolens*), right, cascades onto a path in a large garden. As people brush past the leaves the delicious scent of mint is released.

Dale Harvey

which are often planted as borders. Consider the shape and spread of the plants you choose, whether they are annuals or perennials; is it permanent or will it have to be replanted? It may be difficult to maintain a show of colour throughout the year.

Containing Herbs

Clipped hedges add definition to a formal design and can be particularly good for containing the herbs which tend to wander. Most herbs are rabid self-seeders and also spread by root. Take care not to plant mint, tansy, tarragon or lemon balm straight into the garden. One alternative is to keep these herbs in pots, but beware as the roots can still escape through the holes in the pots and invade your garden. As potted plants they can be

Lamiaceae (Labiatae) -The Mint family

Members of the mint family are widely distributed on every continent, from cool areas through to the tropics, and a very large number are cultivated either as ornamentals or as culinary herbs.

A distinguishing feature of the family is that the stems and leaves are often covered in hairs and glands that contain essential oils which, when released, give off a strong aroma. The stems of members of the family usually are square in shape and the flowers have a distinctive tubular shape. Some of the best known members of the mint family include:

- *Australian mint bushes: Prostanthera species*
- *Bergamots: Monarda species*
- *Bugles: Ajuga species*
- *Catmints: Nepeta species*
- *Lavenders: Lavandula species*
- *Mints: Mentha species*
- *Oreganos or marjorams: Origanum species*
- *Sages: Salvia species*
- *Thymes: Thymus species*

moved around your garden as you see fit.

While herbs were traditionally grown for their medicinal and cosmetic purposes, today we mainly grow them for their culinary uses, and most gardeners use herbs throughout their garden to add colour and fragrance overall. Take away the lavenders, rosemary, chamomiles, santolina, thymes and nasturtiums and many of our favourite garden plants are gone.

Herbs are the easiest of plants to grow, flourishing in most soils. Their only requirements are full sun and good drainage, although there are some, such as the various mints (*Mentha* species), that will survive in a damp or shady position. Such prolific growers, they really make an instant garden. Put them in one season and within months the garden will look well estab-lished. Herbs can be planted to add a purely ornamental touch to a garden as the different tones and textures of the leaves will complement flowers, shrubs and trees.

Easy Access

Accessibility is one of the most important considerations in planning a herb garden for practical use. You may have a suitable garden bed quite close to your kitchen door, if not, try to position a pot or two of the most commonly used herbs just outside the door, or in a windowbox on the kitchen windowsill. If space is limited, plant a herbal walk from the back door to the garage/clothesline/gate. Edge the path with parsley, sage, rosemary, thyme and other favourite herbs so that any strolls down the path will be fragrant ones!

Thyme

Bronze fennel

Lemon balm , thyme and sage.

Rodney Hyett

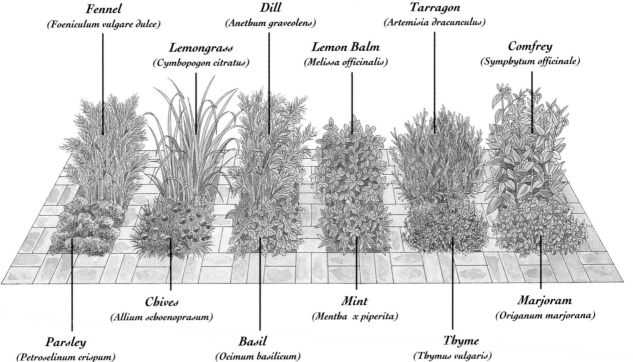

Fennel
(Foeniculum vulgare dulce)

Lemongrass
(Cymbopogon citratus)

Dill
(Anethum graveolens)

Lemon Balm
(Melissa officinalis)

Tarragon
(Artemisia dracunculus)

Comfrey
(Symphytum officinale)

Chives
(Allium schoenoprasum)

Mint
(Mentha x piperita)

Marjoram
(Origanum marjorana)

Parsley
(Petroselinum crispum)

Basil
(Ocimum basilicum)

Thyme
(Thymus vulgaris)

A Herb Ladder

*T*he herb ladder is an ideal way to keep herbs neat and tidy. It allows easy access to all herbs and is a particularly attractive, and practical, beside a pathway.

Here the edges of the ladder are defined by a basketweave pattern of bricks. Other materials such as railway sleepers, cobble stones or sandstone pieces could also be used.

A selection of taller herbs such as fennel, lemongrass, dill, lemon balm, tarragon and comfrey provide a backdrop to the lower growing herbs at the front of the ladder. A collection of parsely, chives, basil, mint, thyme and marjoram produces a carpet of foliage and textures.

Lemongrass

Parsley

Flowering basil

Simon Kenny

Standard Procedures

To train a plant into a standard, simply choose a plant with a straight stem, prune off any side shoots and pinch out the ends of the top growth to promote bushy growth. Use a liquid fertiliser high in nitrogen to promote growth and keep removing side shoots and shaping top until desired size and shape is reached. In dry arid areas, the Mediterranean look - terracotta pots brimming with lavenders, citrus or a bay tree, at right, - works well. Use only a few types of plants and the same style of pots for a unified look. Too many different elements can look unplanned, untidy and unappealing.

The Kitchen Garden

Creating a pretty and productive planting

The scent of ripe tomatoes is enough to convince me that even the utilitarian vegetable garden can be full of aroma. Why not make this productive area of the garden into something beautiful and fragrant as well? Plant scented roses along the fences, sweet peas along a back trellis and add hedges of lavender and rosemary along pathways. The lush greens of lettuces and feathery tops of carrots in neat rows can create quite a pleasing picture. Remember, too, vegetables such as globe or Jerusalem artichokes produce striking flowers.

The late Edna Walling wrote on finally coming to terms with her own vegetable garden. "I think I've got the hang of vegetable growing at last. Apparently you have to do a little messing around in the vegetable garden every day, or at least every other day." This she achieved by planting many of her favourite plants in with the vegetables. "I have started edging the paths with prostrate rosemary, Hypericum and various thymes, and today I straightened my back and beheld a picture composed of the golden blooms of this Hypericum and the quaint little white daisy-flowers of chamomile."

If artistry is the means of enticement into the kitchen garden, try your hand at creating a potager. Originally evolved from the mediaeval monastery garden and then used widely by the French, a potager simply means a kitchen garden of culinary herbs and vegetables. It can be as simple as a square plot divided into triangular beds with symmetrical paths, or as intricate as the Heide garden in Melbourne. Time is all-important. Reconcile how

Kitchen gardens don't need to be vast to feed a family. This charming plot, enclosed with a handmade paling fence is enough for an entire family and still has room for fragrant climbers such as sweet peas, climbing roses and colourful nasturtiums to create a cottage-style garden.
Inset: The sweetly scented orange tree is a welcome addition to a kitchen garden in temperate climates.

Rodney Hyett/Trisha Dixon

much available time you have for such an enterprise and don't just believe that it will take care of itself. Vegetable gardens, more than any other style of garden, require much elbow grease. You need to spend at least a quarter of an hour a day during the growing season in the garden.

Berries and Fruit

If room is not an issue, grow some berries and fruit trees, although make sure that as the trees mature, they will not block sun from the vegetables. If you live in a cold climate, think about enclosing your kitchen garden either with trellis covered with fragrant climbers, a wall or wooden fence. The sense of enclosure is appealing, but it also creates a microclimate which may prolong your growing season. While you cannot change the weather patterns of your area, the establishment of a microclimate provides shade or shelter from the elements, and also creates a warmer or cooler, wetter or drier atmosphere.

Citrus trees have some of the most beautiful perfumes, making them an ideal companion to kitchen gardens. Most fruit trees have scented leaves and some have the most beautifully fragrant blossoms, particularly orange and grapefruit. They need just the right position and a little extra care, but the rewards are more than worth it in terms of fragrance and, of course, the fruit.

If you are seeking inspiration for a romantic fragrant kitchen garden you can visit one of Australia's greatest examples in Victoria. The Heide Kitchen Garden in Bulleen was originally created with great artistry some 70 years ago by Sunday Reed. Totally enclosed by a picket fence, festooned with roses such as 'Fantin Latour', 'Madam Sancy de Parabere', *Rosa multiflora* and fragrant 'Souvenir de la Malmaison', the garden includes some 300 herb, vegetable and flower species and more than 70 species of old-fashioned roses. Runner beans and rows of lettuce are glimpsed through a sea of campion and foxgloves. This national treasure has recently been restored, with its old world atmosphere remaining intact; it is open to the public.

Sprinkling a few flowers through the kitchen garden as an enticement to linger is in evidence in this large country garden. Daffodils, daisies and honesty, top, mingle with decorative lettuces, onions and a vast array of edible vegetables and herbs. The kitchen garden at Heide in Victoria, left, is an inspiration for anyone contemplating a kitchen garden. Enclosed by a paling fence draped with climbing roses, a myriad of paths weave through cleverly planned beds of vegetables, herbs, perennials and roses.

Trisha Dixon/Joe Filshie

Rodney Hyett

Rutaceae - The Rue family

The family was named after the European herb rue (Ruta graveolens), known as the herb of grace. This strongly aromatic herb has been used for centuries for its reputed medicinal properties (although in large doses it can be toxic). Like plants in the Myrtaceae family, the leaves of members of Rutaceae also have very prominent oil glands which release

Lemon blossom.

strong aromas when crushed. The oils can be so potent that one member of the family (of biblical fame) is known as the burning bush (Dictamnus) due to the leaf oil catching on fire on extremely hot days.

As well as fragrant leaves, many members of this family also have perfumed flowers, such as orange blossom. The citrus group is probably the best known of this family in cultivation, but there are many other interesting rutaceous plants for the gardener to become acquainted with. The citrus group generally is characterized by having oil not only in the leaves, but also in the rinds of their fruits. Most of the flowers of the different citruses are fragrant, which is an attraction to any gardener.

Following is a selection from this ornamental and economically important family:

- *Brown boronia* (Boronia megastigma)
- *Correa* species
- *Diosma* (Coleonema pulcrum)
- *Grapefruit* (Citrus paradisi)
- *Lemon* (Citrus limon)
- *Lime* (Citrus aurantifolia)
- *Mandarin* (Citrus reticulata)
- *Mexican orange blossom* (Choisya ternata)
- *Orange* (Citrus sinensis)
- *Orange jessamine or mock orange* (Murraya paniculata)
- *Rose China bush* (Adenandra fragrans): with aniseed-scented leaves & sweetly perfumed flowers
- *Sydney rock rose* (Boronia serrulata)
- *Waxflower* (Eriostemon myoporoides)

Rodney Hyett

Starting a Vegetable Patch

Most fruit and vegetable varieties require full sun, with a well-drained fertile soil. If your soil has particularly poor drainage, creating raised beds could be the solution.

Raised beds can be created using stone or suitable timber (such as railway sleepers or treated pine), built up to a height of 20-30cm (8-12in). The beds can be filled with a mixture of 75 percent topsoil to 25 percent compost. Homemade compost is ideal, but if this is not available then aged animal manure will be equally as good (provided it is reasonably weed-free). Another strategy for your raised beds is to create a "no dig" garden. A thick layer of newspaper (about 15 sheets thick) is placed at the bottom to suppress weed growth. Straw or stable bedding is then added to a depth of 10cm (4in) followed by a 5cm (2in) layer of weed free compost. A further 10cm (4in) of straw is then added and this is capped off by another 5cm (2in)

of compost. Plants are placed straight into the top compost layer and the whole mixture gradually subsides as the straw starts to break down. At the end of the season a new layer of straw and compost can be added to rejuvenate the garden.

Rapid Growth

Whichever growing medium is used, a weekly or fortnightly dose of a complete liquid fertiliser is desirable while plants are being established. A 5cm (2in) layer of mulch such as lawn clippings, manure or shredded paper will help keep moisture in the soil. Be prepared to give your kitchen garden more watering than a normal garden. Fruit and vegetables are bred to grow very rapidly and so require extra water and fertiliser. Most vegetables are annuals and have very definite seasonal requirements for planting and harvesting and these must be adhered to if you wish to achieve good results.

Pest and Disease Control

*F*ruit and vegetables, with their rapid succulent growth are a magnet for pests and diseases. Sucking insects such as aphids, white flies and mites should be monitored as well as chewing insects such as caterpillars and beetles.

Crop rotation (not growing the same crop in the same spot each year) is an excellent way of controlling many diseases. This also extends to crops in the same family; tomatoes, capsicums and potatoes all belong to the Solanceae family and are often affected by the same diseases. Peas and beans are in the legume family, while pumpkins, cucumbers and melon are in the cucurbit family. By rotating these families around the garden we greatly minimise the spread of diseases.

Plant a number of different lettuce varieties, top, for decorative and culinary appeal. A rose-clad pergola makes a colourful backdrop for this vegetable garden, right, growing amidst daisies, Queen Anne's lace and nasturtiums. A hedge of newly planted Buxus will eventually border the neat rows of vegetables which currently includes silverbeet, artichokes, and spring onions.

Leigh Clapp

Formal Culinary
HERB GARDEN

This garden is entered via a wooden arbor adorned with a fragrant climber such as honeysuckle, rose or star jasmine. A topiarised bay tree, underplanted with violets, provides the focal point and forms the central planting bed. It is edged with chamomile and mint which will spill onto the pathway so their scent will be released when trodden on. The com-pacted gravel pathway is edged with a series of ground-hugging herbs including basil, chives and thyme. Behind is an assortment of herbs which increase in height at the corners. Prune to maintain density by regular tip pruning. Defining the garden is a series of clipped lavender and rosemary hedges. In front of the lavender hedge is a wooden bench from which to survey the garden.

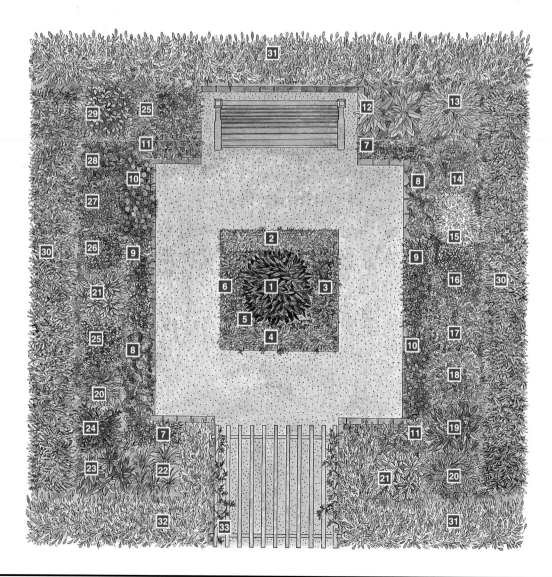

Key for Plan

1. **Bay tree** *(Laurus nobilis)*
2. **English chamomile** *(Anthemis nobilis)*
3. **Peppermint** *(Mentha piperita)*
4. **Lawn chamomile** *(Anthemis nobilis 'Treneague')*
5. **Sweet violets** *(Viola odorata)*
6. **Spearmint** *(Mentha spicata)*
7. **Garden thyme** *(Thymus vulgaris)*
8. **Parsley** *(Petroselinum crispum)*
9. **Lemon thyme** *(Thymus citriodorus)*
10. **Chives** *(Allium schoenoprasum)*
11. **Basil** *(Ocimum basilicum)*
12. **Sorrel** *(Rumex scutatus)*
13. **Fennel** *(Foeniculum vulgare)*
14. **Rue** *(Ruta graveolens)*
15. **Curry plant** *(Helichrysum italicum)*
16. **Lemon verbena** *(Aloysia triphylla)*
17. **Italian parsley** *(Petroselinum crispum)*
18. **Caraway** *(Carum carvi)*
19. **Borage** *(Borago officinalis)*
20. **Dill** *(Anethum graveolens)*
21. **Sage** *(Salvia officinalis)*
22. **Garlic** *(Allium sativum)*
23. **Comfrey** *(Symphytum officinale)*
24. **French tarragon** *(Artemisia dracunculus)*
25. **Oregano** *(Origanum vulgare)*
26. **Marjoram** *(Origanum majorana)*
27. **Coriander** *(Coriandrum sativum)*
28. **Lemon balm** *(Melissa officinalis)*
29. **Lovage** *(Levisticum officinale)*
30. **Rosemary** *(Rosmarinus officinalis)*
31. **French lavender** *(Lavandula dentata)*
32. **Italian lavender** *(Lavandula stoechas)*
33. **Honeysuckle** *(Lonicera splendida)*

Borage

Basil is an annual favoured by cooks. It has white flowers and grows to 60cm (2ft); it will not survive frosts.

Bay tree is a slow-growing tree which can be clipped. Leaves are used for pate, bouquet garni and in casseroles. Grows to 12m (40ft).

Bergamot is a perennial with brightly coloured feathery flowers which are used in salads. Grows to 1m (3ft).

Borage is a self-seeding annual. The leaves taste of cucumber and bright blue flowers can be used in drinks or salads. Grows to 1m (3ft).

Chamomile is a ground-cover with daisy-like flowers which are used for teas and potpourri. Grows up to 1m (3ft).

Chives grow topped with purple blooms and are used in salads. Grows to 25cm (10in).

Comfrey is a tall perennial which can be grown at the compost heap as it is a great compost activator. Grows to 1m (3ft).

Dill is a tall annual with feathery green foliage which can be used in soups, or with potatoes or fish. Seeds can be used in pickles, breads, fish sauces. Grows to 1m (3ft).

Garlic is a bulb with tall circular flowerheads. Slivers of the bulb can be used in roasts, sauces, salad dressings or in butters. Grows to 1m (3ft).

Lavender is a bushy herb with mauve spikes of fragrant blooms throughout summer. Used for potpourri and vinegars. Grows to 1m (3ft).

Lemon balm has bright green foliage with a distinctive lemon aroma and flavour; it is delicious when added to cool drinks and tea. Spreads rapidly. Grows to 1m (3ft).

Lemon verbena is a shrub with fragrant, pointed leaves used in linen sachets and potpourri. Frost tender. Grows to 2m (6ft).

Mint is a perennial that adds flavour to drinks and salads. It spreads rapidly so keep it contained in a pot. Grows to 1m (3ft).

Oregano is a moderately low-growing perennial with leaves that add a touch of spice to pizza or salads.

Parsley is a must for the herb garden – its leaves are rich in vitamin A and C and iron. A self-seeding biennial, it grows to 1m (3ft).

Chives

Rosemary makes a handsome hedge or shrub with its lovely blue flowers and distinctive fragrance. Grows to 1m (3ft).

Sage is a hardy perennial. It has flowers of pink, white, blue or purple; its leaves are used in salads or stuffings. Grows easily from cuttings. Grows to 1m (3ft).

Thyme is a low-growing perennial with flowers in white, pink and mauve. Its leaves are used in salads and in cooking.

Lawns that are heaven scent

- To make your own thyme lawn, prepare soil thoroughly. Incorporate coarse sand if drainage is poor. Eliminate all weeds.

- Place a few large, flat paving stones through the area as stepping stones.

- Plant thyme only – don't include bulbs, pots or ornaments as this will take away from the effect.

- Plant many small pieces of thyme. If buying thyme in pots, upend pot and divide each plant into 10 or 20 rooted pieces which can be potted and nursed and then planted in the ground at 20cm (1in) spaces. Water in well.

- Keep area weed-free while plants are becoming established. Mulching between the plants with lawn clippings or chopped straw will greatly reduce weeds. Once thyme has carpeted the area, there will be too much competition to allow weeds.

- Choose an array of red, purple and mauve thymes. White can make the lawn look too patchy.

- The other beautifully scented lawn is the chamomile lawn, much coveted by true romantics. Smelling of ripe apples when trodden on, it may not be the most practical of groundcovers, but for a small area or in cracks between paving, it is delightful.

- Chamomile lawns date back to Tudor times, when grass lawns were as rare as chamomile lawns are today; grass lawns were not widely sown until the 18th century.

- For a chamomile lawn, prepare the area, rake soil and eliminate any weeds or competition. Sow chamomile seed in early spring. Anthemis nobilis 'Treneague' is the best for lawns with its brilliant green foliage. Scatter seed sparingly, rake in and water with a fine mist. Keep soil moist until seedlings appear. Keep weed free for the first year by mulching until the plants spread and suppress weeds. Set lawnmower to highest level and mow lawn every few months to encourage chamomile plants to thicken.

The sweet violet (*Viola odorata*) has one of the best loved fragrances. Flourishing in sun or shade, the fresh green foliage and quaint blooms produce a lush carpet.

Anthemis nobilis is a flowering groundcover while the true lawn chamomile (*Anthemis nobilis* 'Treneague') is without flowers.

Rodney Hyett/Leigh Clapp/Dale Harvey

Ground Control

Fabulous fragrance under foot

Scented plants do not have to be at nose level for you to enjoy the benefits of fragrance! Consider planting fragrant groundcovers under colourful, but unscented bushes and trees – or even try a fragrant lawn.

Violets are among the most obliging of the fragrant groundcovers with their nostalgic fragrance and beautiful heart-shaped fresh green foliage. They can be invasive, but are also incredibly obliging and hardy, fast growing and easy to care for. Violets can be divided, transplanted and moved without fuss. They can even be pruned with the lawn mower! The most delicately scented is the aptly named, sweet violet (*Viola odorata*) with its violet and white flowers throughout winter and early spring. Another favourite is the Parma violet. Hybrid violets, like pansies, violas and heartsease, have a little perfume.

A strongly fragrant groundcover is pennyroyal (*Mentha pulegium*). A low growing green perennial, it forms a dense mat of foliage which emits a strong peppermint aroma when trodden on. Try growing it in paving around a barbecue area as the fragrance of peppermint complements the aroma of a meal. Valuable, too, are the huge variety of thymes, and the delicate chamomile.

Thyme is the most obliging groundcov providing a rich green tapestry in the most auspicious of soils. Here, it is teamed with bright carmine flowers.

Key for Plan

1 **Chamomile** *(Anthemis nobilis 'Treneague')*

2 **Basil** *(Ocimum basilicum)*

3 **Lemon thyme** *(Thymus citriodorus)*

4 **Oregano** *(Origanum vulgare)*

5 **Pinks** *(Dianthus x hybrida)*

6 **Parsley** *(Petroselinum crispum)*

7 **Chives** *(Allium schoenoprasum)*

8 **Pyrethrum** *(Tanacetum coccineum)*

9 **French lavender** *(Lavandula dentata)*

10 **Rose** *(Rosa 'Constance Spry')*

11 **Rosemary** *(Rosmarinus officinalis)*

12 **Borage** *(Borago officinalis)*

13 **Swan River daisy** *(Brachyscome iberidifolia)*

14 **Mint** *(Mentha piperita)*

15 **Lime** *(Citrus aurantifolia)*

16 **Native violet** *(Viola hederacea)*

17 **Star jasmine** *(Trachelospermum jasminoides)*

18 **Fennel** *(Foeniculum vulgare dulce)*

19 **Lemon grass** *(Cymbopogon citratus)*

20 **Robinia** *(Robinia pseudoacacia)*

21 **Rose geranium** *(Pelargonium graveolens)*

22 **Dill** *(Anethum graveolens)*

23 **Sweet violet** *(Viola odorata)*

24 **Coriander** *(Coriandrum sativum)*

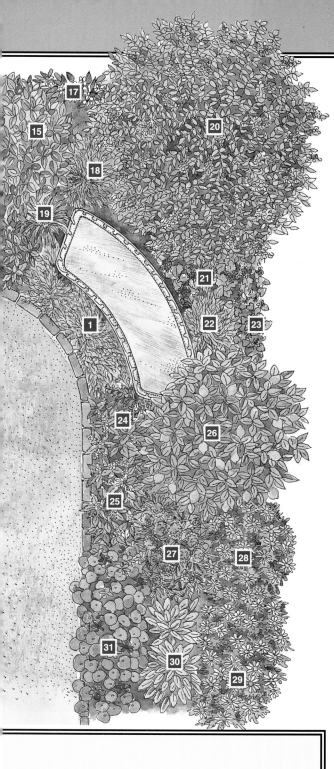

Flower and Herb Corner

Often corners of the garden are neglected. This is an example of how to enhance that space and provide an array of flowers for picking, and a collection of herbs for culinary use.

The design of the stone pathway in this garden allows for chamomile to be planted between the stones. Visitors will tread on and bruise the chamomile leaves, creating a wonderful scent. It is also placed beneath a stone bench to produce the same effect.

Gardens can be places of refuge and in this garden the stone bench allows the visitor to sit and enjoy this fragrant corner. Above the bench a Robinia tree provides shade in the heat of summer as well as allowing through the warm winter sun. Rose geranium is behind the bench, producing a sweet scent when the leaves are crushed. Star jasmine has been trained along the boundary fence and the fence is further softened with climbing roses along its perimeter.

An open lawn is bounded by an array of culinary herbs and plants which increase in height towards the fence. A lime and a lemon tree frame the bench, underplanted with native and sweet violets. Colour is provided by marguerite daisies, marigolds, nasturtiums and lavender.

25 *Catmint* (Nepeta x faassenii)

26 *Lemon* (Citrus limon)

27 *French marigold* (Tagetes patula)

28 *Pink Marguerite daisy* (Chrysanthemum frutescens syn. Argyranthemam frutescens)

29 *White Marguerite daisy* (Chrysanthemum frutescens syn. Argyranthemam frutescens)

30 *Sage* (Salvia officinalis)

31 *Nasturtium* (Tropaeolum majus)

32 *Open lawn*

Hidden Pleasures

Create your own secret scented garden

Rustic timber draped with climbing geraniums leads to a seat positioned by a potted Gardenia.

Within the confines of your garden, create an inner sanctuary, an escape from reality and a fragrant paradise. Such a haven is for the pure romantic and will create an atmosphere of tranquillity and mystery. If you enclose an area, however small, with fragrant climbers, you will ensure seclusion and invite contemplation. A simple but comfortable seat will make the area totally compelling.

While it sounds appealing to have mellowed stone walls surroundng such a sanctuary, this is not always realistic. Grow your own enclosures with hedges of the scented viburnums, buddleias or honeysuckles, or erect a timber trellis and cover with a tapestry of scented climbers such as Clematis, roses and Wisteria. Make sure there are some evergreens among the climbers to ensure a sense of enclosure during winter.

Draped with Colour

A high brick wall can be bagged with lime and draped with a single climbing rose such as the fragrant pink 'Mme Gregoire Staechelin', the creamy white *Rosa devoniensis* or brilliant crimson 'Blackboy'. Rough hewn timber walls or tea-tree fencing can also provide instant privacy. Hedges, on the other hand can take up to five years to reach maturity.

Informality

A more informal secret garden area can be created in an existing garden by simply thickening the boundaries of a garden area or "room". Add evergreen shrubs, trees and tall growing perennials to the borders to achieve a natural boundary. The result will be a romantic haze of foliage in a tapestry of colours, textures and shapes.

The entrance to the secret garden sets the mood for the sanctuary and can be as quixotic and fanciful as wished. The sense of mystery can be heightened by a rustic gate or door, which can even be left ajar to invite exploration. Or an archway draped with fragrant climbers. The entrance needs to be intimate and inviting to ensure a feeling of stepping 'inside'.

Within the secret garden, simplicity is the key. Lawn is the most restful and informal. Complete the theme with a comfortable seat under the canopy of a shady tree or hammock slung between two trees.

A sense of enclosure has been created by an arched brick wall and greenery to camouflage the boundaries.

Uninviting Fragrances

Odious scents are, thankfully, not a usual part of the gardener's milieu. In fact fragrant plants can do much to block out unpleasant odours from outside the garden; especially useful if you live near an abattoir or sewerage works. Even the everyday fumes from a busy city road or nearby factories can be negated with the use of scented screening plants and fragrant climbers at the windows.

While there are literally thousands of plants that can be grown for their sweet fragrance, there are others (very few) that offend! Unpleasant scents can often be foretellers of evil, such as the unpleasant smell of poisonous fungi and the pungent sickly odour of hemlock, a deadly herb. The stinking hellebore (*Helleborus foetidus*) has the most odious smell of decaying meat. It too is poisonous.

Vile Smelling

In my own garden, I have what surely must be the most quirky of all flowers, the dragon lily (*Dranunculus vulgaris*). Intriguing to look at with its leopard-spotted stem and velvet maroon lily bloom, by mid-summer it has produced a vile smelling vulgar (hence the name) spadix. Smelling like rancid meat, it attracts insects in the hordes (such is its game). I certainly would not be without this unusual plant for sheer oddity value.

The ubiquitous privet (*Ligustrum vulgare*) is a justly maligned plant and yet was a popular hedging plant in the past. Incredibly invasive, the sweet pollen which is disliked by so many can bring on severe hay fever.

The blooms of the Mexican orange blossom (*Choisya ternata*) are favoured by flower arrangers for their clusters of white fragrant flowers, however the foliage is less than pleasant. Anyone that has cut back the foliage or dug up suckers will have encountered the pungent aroma.

Bunches of the herb, tansy, (*Tanacetum vulgare*), are often hung at back doors to keep flies and mosquitoes away. No wonder, the pungent, less-than-pleasant aroma is enough to keep all well away! This fern-leafed, very invasive herb is quite attractive in flower with its yellow button heads but is not recommended for growing in the flower garden as it will most certainly take over! It is also said to deter ants, aphids, cabbage worms, chewing beetles, Japanese beetles and squash bugs. Obviously quite an odour! Restrict it to growing in pots.

Contrastingly, plants that are often treasured for their scent, can be too much in an enclosed area. Such a plant is the climbing jasmine (*Jasminum polyanthum*) which will cover a wall in no time. Sweetly scented, it is a little too obliging with its fragrance that scents the air freely with an almost sickly sweet aroma.

Curry plant

Honeysuckle

Mexican orange blossom

'Zephirine Drouhin'

Rodney Hyett/Dale Harvey

Particular Perfumes

Earlier this century, a test was carried out using more than 400 different scents and the conclusion was that there were six main smells: fruity, flowery, resinous, spicy, foul and burnt. Within these categories however, there are a host of other classes. Following is our selection of pleasing scents and flowers.

Almond

Snowdrop (*Galanthus*): *hardy bulb with delicate white flowers.*

Oleander (*Nerium oleander*): *evergreen poisonous shrub.*

Apple

Thuja occidentalis 'Rheingold': *slow growing conifer.*

Irish Juniper (*Juniperus communis*): *evergreen columnar conifer.*

Eriostemon 'Profusion': *compact shrub with masses of white flowers in spring and beautifully scented foliage.*

Apricot

Osmanthus O. fragrans: *winter-flowering elegant evergreen shrub with tiny white flowers.*

Caraway

Caraway thyme: *evergreen groundcover with mauve flowers.*

Chocolate

Chocolate cosmos (*Cosmos atrosanguineus*): *interesting brown daisies with this tempting aroma.*

The Chocolate lily (*Dichopogon fimbriata*): *delicate mauve flowers that taste and smell like chocolate.*

Cloves

Viburnums (*V. carlesii & V. juddii*): *shrub for cooler areas.*

Phlox (*Phlox drummondii*): *hardy perennial.*

Dianthus: *hardy perennial with violet flowers; used for borders.*

Rosa 'Blush Noisette': *lilac pink shrub.*

Stocks (*Matthiola*): *hardy annuals and biennials with bright blooms.*

Curry

Rice flowers (*Ozothamnus and Cassinia*): *shrubs with everlasting heads of flowers and spicy foliage.*

Curry plant, (*Helichrysum serotinum*): *particularly strong scent; small grey leafed plant with yellow flowers.*

Honey

Dwarf apple gum (*Angophora hispoda*): *spectacular creamy flowers in summer with an unmistakable honey-like perfume.*

Eucalyptus *species have lots of bird attracting nectar which also gives off a distinct honey-like smell*

Honeysuckle (*Lonicera*): *old-fashioned shrub or climber.*

Lemon

Lemon scented myrtle (*Backhousia citriodora*): *small tree with one of the most arresting lemon perfumes of all in the leaves.*

Lemon scented gum (*Eucalyptus citriodora*): *large tree which releases its lemon scent after rain.*

Lemon scented tea tree (*Leptospermum petersonii*): *great screening shrub whose foliage can be used to make an interesting tea.*

Lemon thyme (*Thymus x citriodorus*): *groundcover with pale flowers.*

Balm (*Melissa officinalis*): *perennial herb with fragrant leaves.*

Liquorice

Aniseed tree (*Backhousia anisata*): *large Australian shrub suited to warmer climates. Leaves smell strongly of aniseed. Mildly fragrant white flowers in summer.*

Clematis rehderiana 'Sweet Cicely' (*Myrrhis odorata*): *tall herb with lacy flowers.*

Fennel (*Foeniculum vulgare*): *herb with strongly scented hair-like leaves and small yellow flowers in summer.*

Musk

Rosa 'Penelope': *medium shrub with creamy semi-double flowers.*

Rosa 'Paul's Himalayan Musk': *vigorous climber with single blush-pink flowers.*

Myrrh

Rosa 'Constance Spry': *peony shaped pink blooms.*

Peppermint

Eucalyptus nicholii *and other peppermint gums have a strong aroma when the leaves are crushed. Most are medium to large trees.*

Corsican mint (*Mentha requienii*): *herb groundcover with pale mauve blooms.*

Primrose

Crocus: *hardy bulb with yellow, purple or white blooms.*

Tulipa saxatalis: *bulb with bright pink blooms in spring.*

Raspberry

Rosa 'Zephirine Drouhin': *thornless climber with vivid pink blooms.*

Rosa 'Honorine de Brabant': *striped pink old rose.*

Sweet

Jasmine (*Jasminum polyanthum*) *common climbing plant in many temperate gardens.*

Tuberose (*Polianthes tuberosa*): *autumn-flowering bulb-like plant.*

Jonquils (*Narcissus x hybrida*): *hardy bulb.*

Madagascar jasmine (*Stephanotis*): *climbing plant for warmer climates.*

Heartsease (*Viola tricolor*): *herbaceous perennial with tri-coloured blooms of purple and yellow.*

Sweet Rocket (*Hesperis*): *perennial with white and mauve flowers*

Evening Primrose (*Oenothera biennis*): *hardy biennial with yellow flowers.*

Vanilla

Vanilla lily (*Sowerbaea juncea*): *tiny member of the lily family with mauve flowers with a very strong perfume in spring.*

Wisteria: *hardy deciduous climber with mauve sprays of flowers in spring.*

Fragrant Facts

Fragrant flowers are usually light in colour. Not so with roses however, with reds being the most highly scented. Yellow roses are the least scented.

Thick-textured flowers (Magnolias, Gardenias and frangipanis) are often heavily scented.

Fragrance does not always emanate from the flower. It may come from the seeds, bark, foliage, stalk, root or gum sap.

Unfertilised flowers emit the strongest fragrance. Once impregnated, the flower loses its scent.

Lavender growing in poor soil will be far more fragrant than that growing in good soil.

Flowers are less scented during drought and periods of extreme heat.

Bees, butterflies and moths have organs of smell in their antennae.

Someone who has lost their sense of smell is said to be anosmic.

Many flowers that bloom at night turn toward the moon.

The fragrance of jonquils, above, is all the more cherished as there is little else in flower in winter. Another winter delight, the wallflower (*Cheir-anthus cheiri*), right, can be used to scent winter foliage arrangements. Stocks (*Matthiola incana*), below, are a wonderful addition to a flower arrangement.

Rodney Hyett/Dale Harvey/Leigh Clapp

Fragrance in your Home

What better way of enjoying your favourite scented plants than bringing them inside to enjoy. To walk through a room with the sweet freshness of flowers straight from the garden or to have a posy of fragrant flowers by your bedside or at your workplace is like a breath of fresh air. Bathroom, kitchens, hallways and dining rooms, just about any room of the house will benefit from the colour and fragrance of flowers.

Evocative Scents

Many plant fragrances evoke personal reminisces, such as the sweet scent of violets, redolent of childhood or to sink your face into a spray lilac is to recall the spirit of youth. Posies of violets or bunches of jonquils are favourites to take elderly friends or relations in hospital. A warm room will

'Mr. Lincoln'

actually bring out the fragrance in an arrangement, so nothing too pungent for display in a small room.

Secret Messages

To give a bunch of flowers is still one of the most wonderful romantic gestures. Last century, there was added fascination in receiving a bunch of flowers since they were chosen for the secret messages they conveyed. Traditionally, each flower has a meaning: the red rose – love; the white lily – purity; and rosemary, for remembrance. A spray of ivy was an offer of matrimony and to reply with a striped carnation meant refusal, or even worse, a yellow carnation for disdain! Blue violets were cherished, symbolising faithfulness, and lemon Pelargoniums indicated an unexpected meeting. A gift of lavender did not bode well as this flower symbolised distrust; a bunch of yellow lilies signified falsehood.

Fragrant
CUT FLOWERS

As well as providing a regular supply of fragrant flowers for the house, cutting also helps you prune plants. Most woody plants are pruned after flowering anyway, so cutting the flowers off saves you this trouble. In addition cutting flowers from most plants encourages a repeat burst of flowering.

Why not plan ahead and choose plantings so that you will always have fragrant cut flowers for the house. Some of the best choices include:

Freesias *(Freesia refracta)*

This white spring flowering bulb-like plant can be easily naturalized into most gardens. The flowers are great for table arrangements.

❖

Jonquils *(Narcissus x hybrida)*

Of the Narcissus jonquils, these are the most fragrant and provide wonderful cut flowers in late winter/early spring. The variety 'Erlicheer' is very fragrant and very easy to grow.

❖

Trumpet lilies

Lillies sub as Lilium longiflorum and Lilium formosanum are readily grown in the garden and provide spectacular focal points for flower arrangements. L. longiflorum flowers in mid-summer while L. formosanum is at its best in late summer and early autumn. Another bulb for autumn cut flowers is the Belladonna lily (Amaryllis belladonna). It produces metre-high (3ft) stems with strongly fragrant, pink trumpet-shaped flowers.

❖

Gardenias *(all varieties)*

Gardenias provide reasonably short-lived and short-stemmed cut flowers right through the warmer months of the year and are easily grown from cuttings.

❖

Brown boronia *(Boronia megastigma)*

Popular in the cut flower trade, it has unusually coloured flowers that are brown on the outside and yellow on the inside. They can be grown in a very well-drained position with morning sun; they flower in spring.

❖

Carnations *(Dianthus caryophyllus)*

Tens of millions are consumed each year by the cut flower trade. The best carnations for cut flowers are the Sim varieties, which can flower all year round. The intensity of fragrance varies enormously between varieties so it is best to check this when purchasing. Alternatively, cuttings can be taken from the stem bases of a bunch of cut flowers.

❖

Lavenders

Lavender can be used in mixed flower arrangements. For a country kitchen look try a single bunch in a vase.

❖

Stocks *(Matthiola incana)*

are the outstanding choice if you are looking for an annual to grow to use as fragrant cut flowers. The seed can be sown directly into the final position in early autumn for winter flowering.

❖

Roses

The Hybrid Tea varieties such as 'Queen Elizabeth' and 'Mr Lincoln' make wonderful fragrant cut flowers and will bloom in flushes from spring to autumn. Cutting the flowers, particularly in spring, encourages more blooms right through the warmer months.

Sweet Peas *(Lathyrus odoratus)*

This fragrant gem can be readily trained onto a trellis and need not take up much space in the garden.

❖

Daphne *(Daphne odora)*

Another great cut flower for winter when we are most in need of stimulation from nature.

by Angus Stewart

The perfume of the tobacco plant (*Nicotiana alata*) is prominent at night.

Night Scents

Epiphyllum lauii.

There is nothing quite as quixotic as fragrance in the garden on a balmy summer evening. Just the slightest hint of scent is enticement enough to be outside. The purpose of night scents is to attract their nocturnal pollinators such as insects or even bats.

Many flowers are in fact night performers – frangipani, night-scented stock *(Matthiola bicornis),* evening primrose and the tobacco plant *(Nicotiana alata)*. Then there are those that really come to life at sunset, such as the night-scented jasmine *(Cestrum nocturnum)* and the climbing moonflower *(Ipomoea alba)*. These nocturnal plants compensate for their day-time dowdiness by drenching the air with their rich night-time fragrance. The Nicotianas and evening primrose look as though they have wilted by day and transform as the sun goes down to yield a wonderful perfume. Night-scented stock *(Matthiola bicornis)* is drab by day but shines at night when its lilac flowers expand to fill the air with perfume.

The four o'clock plant *(Mirabilis jalapa)* blooms on cue at 4pm; its trumpet-shaped flowers remain open during the night and fade by morning. It is also known as Belle de Nuit, and Marvel of Peru. The moonflower *(Ipomea alba)* has luminous white flowers that perform at night and close in the day. The Crepe Gardenias *(Ervatamia divaricata)* and *(Tabernaemontana coronaria)* are tropical and subtropical small evergreen trees with elegant white flowers which are wonderfully fragrant at night. The giant Burmese honeysuckle *(Lonicera hildebrandiana)*, the largest of the honeysuckles, has large, tubular creamy flowers with fragrance that strenghtens in the evening. For a quirky addition, try the night-flowering cactus *(Epiphyllum oxypetalum)* with its fragrant white flowers that are timed to flower for the full moon.

Buddleias produce perfumes which attract pollinating butterflies and moths.

Rodney Hyett

Common Problems

Some fragrant plants have problems which are particularly associated with the essential oils which give them their uniqueness. In particular, plants such as the butterfly bushes (Buddleias) produce perfumes which attract pollinating moths and butterflies; they lay their eggs and these of course hatch into caterpillars. Some people may prefer to avoid these plants in their garden, although handpicking caterpillars and squashing them is not a difficult proposition. There is an environmentally friendly spray based on a bacterial pathogen (Bacillus thuringiensis) which only affects caterpillars of moths and butterflies and is therefore totally safe for everything else in the garden. Commercial products containing the bacterial spores are readily available to home gardeners under various trade names.

Another problem often associated with fragrant flowers is a fungal disease known as grey mould. Caused by Botrytis cinerea, this fungus grows on the sugary nectar which gives a number of flowers their honey-like perfume. Your local garden centre should stock a suitable fungicide if the problem gets out of hand. Grey mould can be recognised by grey cottonwool-like growth over the flower.

As well as pests which are specific to fragrant plants you can expect visits from some common ones, too.

Simple Pest Control

Aphids are small, usually green in colour and cluster on succulent shoot tips and flower buds. They are a sucking pest and have a particular affinity for roses. Aphids can often be controlled by simply hosing them off the afflicted plant with a strong jet of water or squashing them between finger and thumb.

Mites are microscopic members of the spider group (arachnids) and thus have eight legs. They usually congregate on the under surface of leaves and are most prevalent in summer. Dislodge them with a strong jet of water from the hose; soapy water also deters them. Predatory mites which eat the pests are also available.

White flies can often be spotted by gently whacking the plant and watching for a cloud of tiny white flies. They are a sucking pest and need to build up to very high levels before significant damage occurs. Spray with pyrethrum or a specialised insecticide.

Scale insects are like circular, raised, smooth scabs which form on stem leaves. Gardenias and citrus are particularly prone to them. Rub them off with your finger and thumb, or if there are large numbers, various forms of white oil can be sprayed on to smother them. These are reasonably friendly to the user and the environment.

Thrips are another microscopic pest which can be a problem, particularly in the soft tissues of flowers. They are microscopic insects with elongated, usually brown bodies. Distortion of flowers and buds can often be caused by thrips. They can be identified by taking a sheet of white paper and hitting the flower onto it. If thrips are present they will be easily spotted against the white background. As with aphids, dislodge them with a strong jet of water from the hose, or if the infestation is heavy, consult your local garden centre for a suitable treatment.

Diseases to watch out for in particular are mildews (downy mildew on leaf undersurfaces and powdery on the upper surfaces). These diseases look like cotton wool on the leaves and are fairly difficult to control – consult your local garden centre.

by Angus Stewart

Pests and Diseases

Controlling garden invaders

The best weapon in the fight against pests and diseases is a healthy garden. To sprinkle insecticides and spray with odious herbicides only takes away from the fragrance of a scented garden. Far better to ensure good gardening practices that will auger well for the health and vigour of your plants.

Mulch, compost and sensible watering will do more towards keeping pests and diseases at bay than a host of unpleasant smelling chemicals. Compost and mulch can provide valuable nutrients to the soil and also help structure the soil to benefit healthy growth.

Natural Balance

Soils are naturally depleted as nutrients are used by growing plants. Rather than renew with artificial sources, humus and vital nutrients in the form of compost and manures can redress this balance.

Companion planting is not a new practice, but one that has been used with success for generations. It simply aims to provide the best environment for growth and vigour by selecting 'friendly' plants as neighbours.

Chives around roses are said to deter aphids; marigolds around vegetable patches are believed to repel insects and nematodes and there are many more practical partners. For more details on good companion plants see our combinations on page 86.

A thick layer of mulch, top, is enough to suppress rampant weed growth and retain moisture levels. Parsley in your herb or vegetable garden, right, will help control asparagus beetles. Plant parsley near asparagus, carrots, chives or tomatoes but away from mint.

A to Z of Fragrant Plants

We have concentrated on plants that are suitable for Mediterranean, temperate and subtropical areas. If you live in arid or desert areas you will find many of the plants for Mediterranean climates will be worth trying. Similarly, plants recommended for subtropical and warm temperate areas will also adapt to some extent to the tropics.

Not every plant mentioned may be easily found in retail outlets in every area. However, it will often be possible to track them down through mail-order nurseries which advertise in specialist gardening magazines.

Following are some explanations of the terms used in the table.

WARM TEMPERATE CLIMATES – temperatures rarely, if ever, below freezing.

COOL TEMPERATE CLIMATES – mild (0 to -5C) to severe frosts (-5C to -15C) in winter.

FROST TENDER – damage will be caused by any frost.

MODERATELY FROST HARDY – plants will tolerate light frosts without significant damage.

FROST HARDY – plants will tolerate frosts to -5C without significant damage.

VERY FROST HARDY – plants will tolerate frosts to -10C without significant damage.

GOOD DRAINAGE – when a hole is filled with water it drains within minutes.

MODERATE DRAINAGE – when a hole is filled with water it drains within hours.

POOR DRAINAGE – when a hole is filled with water it drains within days.

PLANT DIMENSIONS - are in metric, then imperial. All dimensions given are approximates only.

by Angus Stewart

Botanic name	Common name	Family	Height x width
Abelia x grandiflora	Abelia	*Caprifoliaceae*	2 x 2m (6 x 6ft)
Acacia podalyriifolia	Queensland silver wattle	*Mimosacaae*	6 x 3 (20 x 10)
Agonis flexuosa	Willow myrtle	*Myrtaceae*	8 x 5 (25 x 16)
Allium sativum	Garlic	*Liliaceae*	1 x 0.3 (3 x 1)
Allium schoenoprasum	Chives	*Liliaceae*	0.3 x 0.2 (1 x 0.5)
Aloysia triphylla	Lemon verbena	*Verbenaceae*	3 x 2 (10 x 6)
Amaryllis belladonna	Belladonna lily	*Amaryllidaceae*	1 x 0.5 (3 x 1.5)
Anethum graveolens	Dill	*Apiaceae*	1 x 0.5 (3 x 1.5)
Anthemis nobilis	Chamomile	*Asteraceae*	0.3 x 0.5 (1 x 1.5)
Azara microphylla	Azara	*Flacourtiaceae*	5 x 5 (16 x 16)
Backhousia anisata	Aniseed myrtle	*Myrtaceae*	12 x 6 (35 x 20)
Backhousia citriodora	Lemon ironwood	*Myrtaceae*	8 x 4 (25 x 13)
Banksia ericifolia	Heath banksia	*Proteaceae*	5 x 3 (16 x 10)
Banksia integrifolia	Coast banksia	*Proteaceae*	10-15 x 5 (30-50 x 16)
Beaumontia grandiflora	Herald's trumpet	*Apocynaceae*	depends on support
Borago officinalis	Borage	*Boraginaceae*	1 x 0.3 (3 x 1)
Boronia megastigma	Brown boronia	*Rutaceae*	1 x 0.5 (3 x 1.5)
Buddleia alternifolia	Butterfly bush	*Buddleiaceae*	3 x 3 (10 x 10)
Buddleia salvifolia	Butterfly bush	*Buddleiaceae*	3 x 3 (10 x 10)
Buxus sempervirens	Box	*Buxaceae*	5 x 5 (16 x 16)
Callistemon citrinus	Bottlebrush	*Myrtaceae*	3 x 2 (10 x 6)
Calonyction aculeatum (Ipomoea alba)	Climbing moonflower	*Convulvulaceae*	depends on support
Carpenteria californica	Carpenteria	*Saxifragaceae*	2 x 2 (6 x 6)
Cercidiphyllum japonicum	Katsura	*Cercidiphyllaceae*	20 x 8 (65 x 25)
Cestrum nocturnum	Night-scented jasmine	*Solanaceae*	4 x 3 (13 x 10)

Plant type	Flower colour	Flowering time	Fragrant parts	Preferred climate & growing notes & special uses
shrub, evergreen	white & pink	summer to autumn	flowers	Temperate climates. Full sun, moderate drainage, frost hardy. Very tough shrub suitable for hedging or screening.
shrub/small tree, evergreen	yellow	late winter	flowers	Temperate to subtropical. Frost free climates, full sun. Resents hard pruning
small tree, evergreen	white	late spring	leaves	Mediterranean to temperate. Tolerates coastal conditions, prefers good drainage. Responds to pruning.
bulb, deciduous	white	summer	leaves & bulb	Mediterranean to temperate. Full sun, good drainage, tolerates heavy frost. Harvest bulbs in late summer. Bulbs used for cookery.
bulb, evergreen	purple	summer	leaves & bulb	Mediterranean to temperate. Full sun, good drainage, frost hardy. Leaves used for cookery.
shrub, deciduous	pale mauve	summer & autumn	leaves	Temperate. Full sun, good drainage, frost tender. Leaves used for cookery and potpourri.
bulb, deciduous	pink or white	autumn	flower	Mediterranean to temperate. Full sun, reasonable drainage, frost hardy. Good cut flower.
annual herb	yellow	summer	leaves & seeds	Mediterranean to temperate. Full sun, medium drainage, frost hardy. Leaves and seeds used in cookery.
perennial herb, evergreen	white & yellow	summer & autumn	leaves	Mediterranean to temperate. Full sun, good drainage, frost hardy. Flowers used to make tea. Plants can be used as a lawn.
large shrub, evergreen	yellow	late winter	leaves	Mediterranean to temperate. Semi-shade, good drainage, half hardy to frost. Unusual vanilla-scented flowers.
small tree, evergreen	white	spring	leaves	Warm temperate to subtropical climates. Full sun to part shade, good drainage, frost tender. Leaves can be used to make a refreshing tea.
small tree, evergreen	white	early summer	leaves	Temperate to subtropical. Full sun, moderate drainage, frost tender. Leaves have a very strong lemon scent and can be used to make a refreshing tea.
large shrub, evergreen	orange	winter to spring	flowers	Temperate to subtropical. Full sun, tolerates poor drainage, half hardy to frost. Flowers have a honey perfume and are attractive to birds.
small tree, evergreen	yellow	winter	flowers	Mediterranean to temperate & subtropical. Full sun, good drainage, frost hardy. Flowers have a honey perfume and are attractive to birds.
climber, evergreen	white	spring	flowers	Subtropical to tropical. Full sun, good drainage, frost tender. Very large trumpet-shaped flowers.
annual herb	blue	spring & summer	leaves	Mediterranean to temperate. Full sun, good drainage, frost hardy. Leaves are added to drinks, e.g. fruit punch.
shrub, evergreen	brown & yellow	late winter to spring	flowers & leaves	Mediterranean to temperate. Full sun, perfect drainage, frost hardy. Wonderful cut flower.
shrub, deciduous to semi-evergreen	mauve	early summer	flowers	Cool temperate. Full sun, good drainage, frost hardy.
shrub, evergreen	mauve with orange throat	late winter to early spring	flowers	Temperate to subtropical. Full sun, good drainage, frost tender.
shrub, evergreen	yellow-green	late spring	leaves	Mediterranean to temperate. Full sun, good drainage, frost hardy. Leaves have a slight fragrance.
shrub, evergreen	red	spring	leaves	Mediterranean, temperate & subtropical. Full sun, tolerates poor drainage, frost hardy. Responds well to pruning.
climber, evergreen	white	summer	flowers	Subtropical to tropical. Full sun, good drainage, very frost tender. Large flowers that open at night.
shrub, evergreen	white with yellow centre	summer	flowers	Mediterranean and temperate. Full sun, moderate drainage, frost tender.
tree, deciduous	red	spring	flowers	Cool temperate. Full sun, good drainage, half hardy to frost. Autumn leaves are colourful in cool climates.
shrub, evergreen	cream	summer to autumn	flowers	Mediterranean, temperate and subtropical. Full sun, good drainage, frost tender.

111

Botanic name	Common name	Family	Height x width	Plant type	Flower colour	Flowering time
Cheiranthus cheiri	Wallflower	Brassicaceae	0.5 x 0.3m (1.5 x 1) ft	perennial	various	spring to summer
Chimonanthus praecox	Wintersweet (Allspice)	Calycanthaceae	2.5 x 3 (8 x 10)	shrub, deciduous	yellow	winter
Choisya ternata	Mexican orange blossom	Rutaceae	2 x 2 (6 x 6)	shrub, evergreen	white	spring
Citrus reticulata	Mandarin	Rutaceae	4 x 3 (13 x 10)	small tree, evergreen	white	spring
Clematis aristata	Clematis	Ranunculaceae	5 x 3 (16 x 10)	climber	creamy-white	spring
Clematis armandii	Clematis	Ranunculaceae	4-5 x 3 (13-16 x 10)	climber, evergreen	white	spring
Clematis montana	Clematis	Ranunculaceae	10 x 3 (30 x 10)	climber, evergreen	white to pink	spring
Clerodendrum bungei	Clerodendrum	Verbenaceae	2 x 2 (6 x 6)	shrub, evergreen or deciduous	reddish-pink	late summer/ early autumn
Clerodendrum trichotomum	Clerodendrum	Verbenaceae	3 x 3 (10 x 10)	shrub, deciduous	white	late summer/ mid-autumn
Coleonema album	Diosma	Rutaceae	1.5 x 2 (5 x 6)	shrub, evergreen	white	late winter to spring
Convallaria majalis	Lily of the valley	Liliaceae	0.3 x 2 (1 x 6)	perennial, rhizomatous	white	spring
Cordyline australis	Cabbage tree	Agavaceae	10 x 5 (30 x 16)	small tree, evergreen	white	spring
Crowea species	Crowea	Rutaceae	1-1.5 x 0.5 (3 - 5 x 1.5)	shrub, evergreen	pink	autumn
Cymbopogon citratus	Lemongrass	Poaceae	1.5 x 1 (5 x 3)	perennial herb	white	summer
Cyclamen purpurascens	Cyclamen	Primulaceae	0.1 x 0.3 (0.5 x 1)	tuber, deciduous	reddish-purple	summer to autumn
Daphne odora	Daphne	Thymeleaceae	1.5 x 1 (5 x 3)	shrub, evergreen	white to purple	winter to spring
Darwinia citriodora	Lemon-scented myrtle	Myrtaceae	1 x 1 (3 x 3)	shrub, evergreen	yellow and red	mid-winter to spring
Datura (Brugmansia) candida	Angels' trumpet	Solanaceae	4 x 3 (13 x 10)	shrub, evergreen	white	summer to autumn
Datura (Brugmansia) chlorantha	Angels' trumpet	Solanaceae	4 x 2 (13 x 6)	shrub, evergreen	creamy-yellow	summer to autumn
Datura (Brugmansia) sanguinea	Angels' trumpet	Solanaceae	4 x 3 (13 x 10)	shrub, evergreen	orange-red	autumn to winter
Datura (Brugmansia) suaveolens	Angels' trumpet	Solanaceae	3 x 3 (10 x 10)	shrub, evergreen	white double	autumn to winter
Dianthus plumarius	Pinks	Caryophyllaceae	0.5 x 0.3 (1.5 x 1)	perennial, evergreen	white to pink to purple	spring
Dianthus `Mrs Sinkins'	Pinks	Caryophyllaceae	0.5 x 0.3 (1.5 x 1)	perennial, evergreen	white	spring
Dianthus `Old English Mauve'	Pinks	Caryophyllaceae	0.5 x 0.3 (1.5 x 1)	perennial, evergreen	mauve	spring
Dichopogon fimbriatus	Chocolate lily	Liliaceae	0.5 x 0.5 (1.5 x 1.5)	perennial, soft-wooded	blue to violet	spring
Drancuculus vulgaris	Dragon lily	Araceae	1 x 0.5 (3 x 1.5)	perennial, deciduous tuber	purple	spring to summer
Eleocarpus reticulatus	Blueberry ash	Elaeocarpaceae	10 x 5 (30 x 16)	small tree, evergreen	white or pink	spring
Epiphyllum oxypetalum	Night-flowering cactus	Cataceae	2 x 1 (6 x 3)	perennia,l soft-wooded	white	spring to summer
Eriostemon myoporoides	Waxflower	Rutaceae	2 x 1 (6 x 3)	shrub, evergreen	white	spring

Fragrant parts	Preferred climate & growing notes & special uses
flowers	Mediterranean and temperate. Full sun, good drainage, frost hardy. Good cut flower.
flowers	Temperate. Full sun, good drainage, half hardy to frost.
flowers & leaves	Mediterranean, temperate and subtropical. Full sun, good drainage, half hardy to frost. Member of citrus family.
flowers & leaves	Mediterranean, temperate and subtropical. Full sun, good drainage, frost tender. Good container plant with edible fruits.
flowers	Temperate and subtropical. Full sun to light shade, good drainage, half hardy to frost.
flowers	Cool temperate. Full sun, good drainage, frost hardy. Prune immediately after flowering.
fowers	Mediterranean, temperate and subtropical. Full sun, good drainage, frost hardy. Prune immediately after flowering.
flowers	Mediterranean, temperate and subtropical. Semi-shade,good drainage, frost tender. A vigorous shrub which suckers.
flowers	Mediterranean, temperate and subtropical. Full sun,good drainage, frost hardy. Bright blue berries follow flowers in winter.
leaves	Mediterranean, warm temperate and subtropical. Full sun, good drainage, frost tender. Stands hard pruning and makes an excellent hedge.
flowers	Mediterranean to cool temperate. Semi-shade, good drainage, frost hardy. Beautiful cut flower.
flowers	Mediterannean, temperate and subtropical. Full sun, good drainage, frost tender. Good for seaside.
flowers	Temperate. Full sun, perfect drainage, moderately frost hardy. Great cut flowers.
leaves	Temperate climates. Full sun, good drainage, frost hardy. Leaves used for culinary purposes.
flowers	Cool temperate. Part-shade, good drainage, moderately frost hardy. Silver-patterned leaves.
flowers	Temperate. Part-shade good drainage, moderately frost hardy. Prefers an acidic pH (5-5.5). Prone to root rot.
leaves	Mediterranean to temperate. Full sun to part-shade, tolerates poor drainage, frost tender.
flowers	Warm temperate to subtropical. Full sun, good drainage, frost tender. Scent is strongest at night. Poisonous if any part of the plant is ingested.
flowers	Warm temperate to subtropical. Full sun, good drainage, mildly frost hardy. Poisonous if any part of the plant is ingested.
flowers (mildly fragrant)	Warm temperate to subtropical. Full sun, good drainage, frost tender. Scent is strongest at night. Poisonous if any part of the plant is ingested.
flowers	Warm temperate to subtropical. Full sun, good drainage, frost tender. Scent is strongest at night. Poisonous if any part of the plant is ingested.
flowers	Mediterranean to cool temperate. Full sun, good drainage, frost hardy. Superb cut flower.
flowers	Mediterranean to cool temperate. Full sun, good drainage, frost hardy. Superb cut flower.
flowers	Mediterranean to cool temperate. Full sun, good drainage, frost hardy. Superb cut flower.
flowers	Mediterranean to temperate climates. Full sun, good drainage, frost hardy. Flowers have a chocolate perfume. Good for rockeries. Not widely cultivated.
flowers	Temperate. Full sun, good drainage, moderately frost hardy. Clumping plant with interesting lobed, glossy leaves. Flower gives off unpleasant odour similar to rotting flesh.
flowers	Warm temperate to subtropical climates. Full sun to part-shade, good drainage, frost tender. Aniseed-scented flowers followed by beautiful blue berries.
flowers	Mediterranean to dry temperate climates. Full to part-sun, good drainage, frost tender. Flowers come out at night. A good plant for drier climates.
leaves	Mediterranean to temperate. Full sun, good drainage, moderately frost hardy.

Clematis armandii

Darwinia citriodora

Eleocarpus reticulatus

Eriostemon myoporoides

Rodney Hyett/Angus Stewart

113

Hymenosporum flavum

Hesperis matronalis

Botanic name	Common name	Family	Height x width
Ervatamia (Tabernaemontana) divaricata	Crepe gardenia	*Apocynaceae*	2.5 x 2m *(8 x 6)ft*
Eucalyptus citriodora	Lemon-scented gum	*Myrtaceae*	30 x 10 *(100 x 30)*
Eucalyptus nicholii	Peppermint gum	*Myrtaceae*	20 x 10 *(65 x 30)*
Eucryphia glutinosa	Eucryphia	*Eucryphiaceae*	10 x 8 *(30 x 25)*
Eucryphia lucida	Leatherwood	*Eucryphiaceae*	10 x 5 *(30 x 16)*
Fortunella japonica	Cumquat	*Rutaceae*	3 x 3 *(10 x 10)*
Freesia alba (F.refracta, 'Alba')	White freesia	*Iridaceae*	0.3 x 0.1 *(1 x 0.5)*
Galanthus nivalis	Snowdrop	*Amaryllidaceae*	0.3 x 0.1 *(1 x 0.5)*
Gardenia augusta	Gardenia	*Rubiaceae*	1.5 x 1.5 *(5 x 5)*
Gardenia augusta 'Grandiflora' & 'Magnifica'	Gardenia	*Rubiaceae*	2 x 1.5 *(6 x 5)*
Gardenia augusta 'Radicans'	Gardenia	*Rubiaceae*	0.5 x 1.5 *(1.5 x 5)*
Gelsemium sempervirens	Carolina jasmine	*Loganiaceae*	depends on support
Hamamelis mollis	Chinese witch hazel	*Hamamelidaceae*	5 x 4 *(16 x 13)*
Hedychium coronarium	White ginger lily	*Zingiberaceae*	1.5 x 1 *(5 x 3)*
Hedychium gardnerianum	Kahili ginger	*Zingiberaceae*	1.5 x 1 *(5 x 3)*
Helichrysum serotinum (H. italicum)	Curry plant	*Asteraceae*	0.5 x 1 *(1.5 x 3)*
Helleborus foetidus	Stinking hellebore	*Ranunculaceae*	0.5 x 0.5 *(1.5 x 1.5)*
Hesperis matronalis	Sweet rocket	*Brassicaceae*	1 x 0.5 *(3 x 1.5)*
Hymanocallis x festalis	Spider lily	*Amaryllidceae*	1 x 0.5 *(3 x 1.5)*
Hymenosporum flavum	Native or Australian frangipani	*Pittosporaceae*	10 x 5 *(30 x 16)*
Iris albicans	Flag iris	*Iridaceae*	0.5 x 0.5 *(1.5 x 1.5)*
Jasminum azoricum	Jasmine	*Oleaceae*	1.5 x 2 *(5 x 6)*
Jasminum mesneyi	Primrose jasmine	*Oleaceae*	3 x 3 *(10 x 10)*
Jasminum officinale	Jasmine	*Oleaceae*	depends on support
Jasminum polyanthum	Jasmine	*Oleaceae*	depends on support

Plant type	Flower colour	Flowering time	Fragrant parts	Preferred climate & growing notes & special uses
shrub, evergreen	white	summer	flowers	Tropical to subtropical. Full sun, good drainage, very frost tender. Very fragrant at night.
tree, evergreen	white	winter	leaves	Mediterranean to temperate. Full sun, good drainage, frost hardy. Very fragrant after rain. Mature trees are prone to dropping large branches.
tree, evergreen	white	autumn	leaves	Mediterranean to temperate. Full sun, good drainage, frost hardy.
tree, deciduous	white	late summer	flowers	Cool temperate. Full sun, moderate drainage, moderately frost hardy. Protect from strong winds. Prefers acidic soils.
tree, evergreen	white	summer	flowers	Cool temperate. Full sun, moderate drainage, moderately frost hardy. Protect from strong winds. Prefers acidic soils.
small tree, evergreen	white	spring	flowers & leaves	Mediterranean, temperate and subtropical. Full sun, good drainage, frost tender. Good container plant with edible fruits.
corm, deciduous	white	late winter-spring	flowers	Mediterranean to warm temperate. Full sun to part-shade, frost tender. Good for naturalising under trees and in lawns in warmer climates. Good cut flower.
bulb, deciduous	white	late winter	flowers	Mediterranean to temperate. Partial shade, moderate drainage, frost hardy. Good for naturalising in suitable climates.
shrub, evergreen	white	spring to autumn	flowers	Mediterranean to temperate. Light shade, good drainage, frost tender. Attractive, glossy foliage. Good cut flower.
shrub, evergreen	white	spring to autumn	flowers	Mediterranean to temperate. Light shade, good drainage, frost tender. Grandiflora similar to Augusta but has double flowers and the plant is a little larger.
shrub, evergreen	white	spring to autumn	flowers	Mediterranean to temperate. Light shade, good drainage, frost tender. A ground covering form of Gardenia useful for confined spaces.
climber, evergreen	yellow	spring to summer	flowers	Temperate climates. Full sun, good drainage, slightly frost tender.
shrub, deciduous	yellow	winter	flowers	Cool temperate climates. Full sun, good drainage, very frost tolerant. Flowers on bare branches before leaves appear. Highly fragrant. Best in cool climates.
perennial, rhizomatous (clumping)	white	summer to autumn	flowers	Warm temperate to subtropical climates. Full sun, moderate drainage, frost tender. Makes a good cut flower. Easily multiplied by division of clumps in spring.
perennial, rhizomatous (clumping)	yellow & red	autumn	flowers	Warm temperate to subtropical climates. Full sun, moderate drainage, frost tender. Makes a very interesting cut flower. Easily multiplied by division of clumps in spring.
small shrub, evergreen	yellow	summer	leaves	Mediterannean to temperate. Full sun, good drainage, frost hardy. Interesting silvery-grey foliage which has a spicy, curry-like perfume. A good groundcover.
perennial, evergreen	green	late winter	flowers	Mediterannean to temperate. Partial to deep shade, good drainage, frost hardy. Good for planting under trees. Very unusual fragrance. Interesting foliage.
perennial, evergreen	white	summer	flowers	Mediterranean to cool temperate. Full sun, good drainage, frost hardy. Fragrant only at night. Leaves can be used in salads.
bulb, deciduous	white	spring	flowers	Temperate climates. Part-shade, good drainage, frost tender. Dies down in winter. Sweet perfume.
tree, evergreen	yellow	spring	flowers	Warm temperate climates. Full sun, good drainage, frost tender. Prefers acidic soils. Pyramidal in shape.
perennial, rhizomatous (clumping)	white & yellow	summer	flowers	Warm temperate climates. Full sun, good drainage, frost tender. Can be increased by dividing clumps in autumn.
climber or groundcover, evergreen	white	spring-summer	flowers	Warm temperate climates. Full sun, good drainage, frost tender. Prune after flowering. Sprawling plant which can also be used as a groundcover.
sprawling shrub, evergreen	yellow	spring	flowers	Warm temperate climates. Full sun, good drainage, frost tender. Perfume delicate.
climber, semi-evergreen	white with pink buds	summer	flowers	Temperate climates. Full sun, good drainage, moderately frost hardy. Plants are fully deciduous in cooler climates.
climber, evergreen	white with pink buds	spring	flowers	Warm temperate climates. Full sun to light shade, good drainage, frost tender. Can be very invasive and weedy if allowed to spread unchecked.

Botanic name	Common name	Family	Height x width	Plant type	Flower colour	Flowering time
Jasminum rex	Jasmine	*Oleaceae*	depends on support	climber, evergreen	white	spring
Juniperus communis	Irish juniper	*Cupressaceae*	3-15 x 1-4m *(10-50 x 3-13)ft*	shrub/ small tree, evergreen	n/a	n/a
Lathyrus odoratus	Sweet pea	*Fabaceae*	depends on support	climber, annual	white to pink to purple	winter to spring
Laurus nobilis	Bay laurel	*Lauraceae*	12 x 10 *(35 x 30)*	smalll tree, evergreen	yellow	spring
Lavandula angustifolia	English lavender	*Lamiaceae*	1 x 0.5 *(3 x 1.5)*	shrub, evergreen	mauve	late spring to early summer
Lavandula angustifolia 'Alba'	White English lavender	*Lamiaceae*	1 x 0.5 *(3 x 1.5)*	shrub, evergreen	white	late spring to early summer
Lavandula angustifolia 'Rosea'	Pink English lavender	*Lamiaceae*	1 x 0.5 *(3 x 1.5)*	shrub, evergreen	pink	late spring to early summer
Lavandula dentata	French lavender	*Lamiaceae*	1.5 x 0.5 *(5 x 1.5)*	shrub, evergreen	mauve	winter to spring
Lavandula stoechas	Italian lavender	*Lamiaceae*	1 x 0.5 *(3 x 1.5)*	shrub, evergreen	purple	late spring to early summer
Lavandula viridis	Green lavender	*Laminaceae*	0.5 x 0.5 *(1.5 x 1.5)*	shrub, evergreen	green	spring & summer
Leptospermum petersonii	Lemon-scented tea tree	*Myrtaceae*	4 x 3 *(13 x 10)*	shrub, evergreen	white	summer
Lilium auratum	Oriental lily	*Liliaceae*	1-2 x 0.5 *(3-6. x 1.5)*	bulb, deciduous	white	summer
Lilium candidum	Madonna lily	*Liliaceae*	1.5 x 0.3 *(5 x 1)*	bulb, deciduous	white	summer
Lilium longiflorum	White trumpet lily	*Liliaceae*	1 x 3 *(3 x 10)*	bulb, deciduous	white	summer
Lomandra longifolia	Spiny mat-rush	*Xanthorrho-eaceae*	1 x 1 *(3 x 3)*	perennial, rhizomatous	yellow	spring
Lonicera fragrantissima	Winter honeysuckle	*Caprifoliaceae*	2 x 4 *(6 x 13)*	shrub, semi-evergreen to deciduous	white	winter
Lonicera hildebrandiana	Giant Burmese honeysuckle	*Caprifoliaceae*	depends on support	climber, deciduous	creamy-yellow	summer
Lonicera japonica	Honeysuckle	*Caprifoliaceae*	depends on support	climber, evergreen	white	late summer to autumn
Luculia grandifolia	Luculia	*Rubiaceae*	4 x 4 *(13 x13)*	shrub, evergreen	white	summer
Luculia gratissima	Luculia	*Rubiaceae*	3 x 1.5 *(10 x 5)*	shrub, evergreen	pink	winter to spring
Lupinus arboreus	Tree lupin	*Fabaceae*	2 x 1.5 *(6 x 5)*	shrub, semi-evergreen	yellow	summer
Magnolia x soulangeana	Magnolia	*Magnoliaceae*	5 x 5 *(16 x 16)*	small tree, deciduous	purple	late spring to early summer
Magnolia quinquepeta 'Nigra'	Lily flowered magnolia	*Magnoliaceae*	4 x 4 *(13 x 13)*	small tree, deciduous	purple	spring
Mandevillea suaveolens	Chilean jasmine	*Apocynaceae*	depends on support	climber, semi-evergreen	white	summer
Matthiola bicornis	Night-scented stock	*Brassicaceae*	0.5 x 0.5 *(1.5 x 1.5)*	annual	lilac	winter & spring
Matthiola incana	Stock	*Brassicaceae*	0.5-1 x 0.3 *(1.5-3 x 1)*	annual	white to pink to purple	winter & spring
Melia azedarach	White cedar	*Meliaceae*	12 x 8 *(35 x 25)*	small tree, deciduous	mauve	spring
Melissa officinalis	Lemon balm	*Lamiaceae*	0.3-0.5 x 1 *(1-1.5 x 3)*	perennial, evergreen	white	summer

Fragrant parts	Preferred climate & growing notes & special uses
flowers	Warm temperate climates. Full sun, good drainage, frost tender. Rather sparse in its growth habit but sweetly fragrant.
leaves	Temperate climates. Full sun, good drainage, frost hardy. There are many different varieties from prostrate groundcovers to column-shaped small trees.
flowers	Mediterranean to temperate climates. Full sun, good drainage, frost hardy. Seed sown in spring to summer. Some form of support is needed.
leaves	Mediterranean to temperate climates. Full sun, good drainage, moderately frost hardy. Good tub plant. Leaves used in cooking. Can be readily shaped by pruning.
leaves	Cool temperate climates. Full sun, good drainage, frost hardy. Highly valued for perfume production.
leaves	Cool climates. Full sun, good drainage, frost hardy. Highly valued for perfume production.
leaves	Cool temperate climates. Full sun, good drainage, frost hardy. Highly valued for perfume.
leaves	Temperate climates. Full sun, good drainage, frost hardy. Useful for potpourri.
leaves	Mediterranean to temperate climates. Full sun, good drainage, frost hardy. Silver grey foliage.
leaves	Cool temperate climates. Full sun, good drainage, frost hardy. Unusual flower colour.
flowers	Mediterranean to temperate and subtropical climates. Full sun, good drainage, moderately frost hardy. Responds well to pruning.
flowers	Temperate climates. Semi-shade, good drainage, frost hardy. Good cut flower.
flowers	Temperate climates. Semi-shade, good drainage, frost hardy. Good cut flower.
flowers	Temperate climates. Semi-shade, good drainage, frost hardy. Good cut flower.
flowers	Temperate to subtropical climates. Full sun to light shade, good drainage, frost hardy.
flowers	Mediterranean to temperate climates. Full sun, good drainage, frost hardy. Dense clumping shrub with honey-like fragrance. Deciduous in cooler climates.
flowers	Mediterranean to cool temperate climates. Semi-shade, good drainage, frost hardy. Honey-scented.
flowers	Temperate climates. Full sun, good drainage. Moderately frost hardy.
flowers	Mediterranean to warm temperate climates. Full sun, very good drainage, frost tender. Prune lightly straight after flowering.
flowers	Mediterranean to warm temperate climates. Full sun, very good drainage, frost tender. Prune lightly straight after flowering.
flowers	Mediterranean to temperate. Full sun, good drainage, frost hardy. A short-lived shrub.
flowers	Mediterranean to temperate climates. Full sun, good drainage, very frost hardy. There are a number of different colour forms from white to purple.
flowers	Mediterranean to temperate climates. Full sun, good drainage, very frost hardy.
flowers	Temperate climates. Light shade, good drainage, moderately frost tolerant. Provide support.
flowers	Mediterranean to temperate climates. Full sun, good drainage, moderately frost tolerant. Sow seed in autumn. Small flowers are highly perfumed at night.
flowers	Mediterranean to temperate climates. Full sun, good drainage, moderately frost tolerant. Sow seeds in autumn. Yields a large number of wonderful cut flowers. Prefers neutral soil pH.
flowers	Temperate to subtropical climates. Full sun, good drainage, frost hardy. Orange berries follow flowers.
leaves	Mediterranean to temperate climates. Full sun, good drainage, frost tolerant. Leaves are used for cooking. Plant spreads by runners and can be invasive. Easily multiplied by dividing clumps.

Lavandula stoechas

Matthiola incana

Melissa officinalis

Rodney Hyett/Leigh Clapp

Nicotiana alata

Michelia figo

Michelia doltsopa

Rodney Hyett/Dale Harvey

Botanic name	Common name	Family	Height x width
Mentha pulegium	Pennyroyal	*Lamiaceae*	0.5 x 1m (1.5 x 3) ft
Mentha requienii	Peppermint (Corsican mint)	*Lamiaceae*	0.5 x 1 (1.5 x 3)
Michelia doltsopa	Michelia	*Magnoliaceae*	10 x 10 (30 x30)
Michelia figo (syn. fuscata)	Port wine magnolia	*Magnoliaceae*	3 x 3 (10 x 10)
Mirabilis jalapa	Four o'clock plant	*Nyctaginaceae*	1 x 0.6 (3 x 2)
Monarda didyma	Bergamot	*Lamiaceae*	1 x 0.3 (3 x 1)
Murraya paniculata	Orange jessamine	*Rutaceae*	2.5 x 3 (8 x 10)
Myrrhis odorata	Sweet cicely	*Apiaceae*	1 x 0.5 (3 x 1.5)
Myrtus communis	Myrtle	*Myrtaceae*	3 x 3 (10 x 10)
Narcissus 'Erlicheer', Paper Whites','Yellow Cheerfulness'	Jonquil	*Amaryllidaceae*	0.3-0.5 x 0.1 (1-1.5 x 0.5)
Nepeta x faassenii	Catmint	*Lamiaceae*	0.5 x 0.5 (1.5 x 1.5)
Nerium oleander	Oleander	*Apocynaceae*	4 x 3 (13 x 10)
Nicotiana alata	Tobacco plant	*Solanaceae*	1 x 0.3 (3 x 1)
Nymphaea odorata 'Alba'	Waterlily	*Nymphaeaceae*	0 x 1 (0 x 3)
Nymphaea odorata 'Minor'	Waterlily	*Nymphaeaceae*	0 x 1 (0 x 3)
Ocimum basilicum	Basil	*Lamiaceae*	0.5 x 0.3 (1.5 x 1)
Oenothera biennis	Evening primrose	*Onagraceae*	1.5 x 0.6 (5 x 2)
Origanum vulgare	Oregano	*Lamiaceae*	0.5 x 0.5 (1.5 x 1.5)
Osmanthus fragrans	Osmanthus	*Oleaceae*	4 x 4 (13 x 13)
Osmanthus heterophyllus	Osmanthus	*Oleaceae*	2.5 x 2.5 (8 x 8)
Pelargonium capitum	Rose-scented geranium	*Geraniaceae*	0.5 x 0.3 (1.5 x 1)
Pelargonium crispum	Lemon-scented geranium	*Geraniaceae*	1 x 0.5 (3 x 1.5)
Pelargonium limonium	Lemon-scented geranium	*Geraniaceae*	1 x 0.5 (3 x 1.5)
Petroselinum crispum	Parsley	*Apiaceae*	0.3 x 0.3 (1 x 1)
Phebalium squameum	Phebalium	*Rutaceae*	3 x 2 (10 x 6)

Plant type	Flower colour	Flowering time	Fragrant parts	Preferred climate & growing notes & special uses
perennial, evergreen	purple	summer	leaves	Mediterranean to temperate climates. Full sun, good drainage, frost tolerant. Leaves used for cooking. Plant spreads by runners and can be invasive. Easily multiplied by dividing clumps.
perennial, semi-evergreen	purple	summer	leaves	Mediterranean to temperate climates. Semi-shade, good drainage, frost tolerant. Plant spreads by runners, can be invasive. Easily multiplied by dividing clumps.
tree, evergreen	creamy-white	late winter to spring	flowers	Mediterranean to warm temperate climates. Full sun, good drainage, frost tender. Prefers an acidic soil pH (5.5).
shrub, evergreen	purple & white	spring	flowers	Mediterranean to warm temperate climates. Full sun, good drainage, frost tender.
perennial, soft-wooded	pink to purple to white	summer	flowers	Warm temperate to subtropical climates. Full sun, good drainage, frost tender. Showy flowers open in late afternoon.
perennial, herbaceous	pink to red	summer	leaves	Mediterranean to temperate climates. Full sun, good drainage, frost hardy. Leaves used in cooking. Also known as bee balm for its ability to attract bees.
shrub, evergreen	white	summer	flowers	Warm temperate climate. Full sun, good drainage, frost tender. Prune after flowering.
perennial, herb	white	summer	leaves & flowers	Mediterranean to cool temperate climates. Full sun, good drainage, very frost hardy. Flowers have an aniseed scent. Leaves and flowers used in cookery.
shrub, evergreen	white	spring to summer	leaves & flowers	Mediterranean to temperate climates. Full sun, good drainage, frost hardy. Leaves used in cookery.
bulb, deciduous	white to yellow	winter to spring	flowers	Mediterranean to temperate climates. Full sun, good drainage, frost hardy.
perennial, soft-wooded	mauve	summer	leaves	Mediterranean to temperate climates. Full sun, good drainage, very frost hardy. An excellent hard groundcover.
shrub, evergreen	white to pink to red	spring to autumn	flowers	Mediterranean to temperate climates. Full sun, good drainage, frost tender. Drought tolerant plant with poisonous leaves and flowers. Tolerates hard pruning.
perennial, soft-wooded	white	summer	flowers	Temperate climates. Full sun, good drainage, frost tender. Flowers fragrant at night.
perennial, deciduous	white	summer	flowers	Temperate climates. Full sun, frost hardy. Plants grow floating in water. Plants should be divided every 3-4 years to retain vigour.
perennial, deciduous	white	summer	flowers	Temperate climates. Full sun, frost hardy. Plants grow floating in water. Plants should be divided every 3-4 years to retain vigrour.
annual	white	summer	leaves	Warm temperate climates. Full sun, good drainage, frost tender. Widely used as a culinary herb and also reputed to have aphrodisiac effects.
biennial	yellow	summer	flowers	Mediterranean to temperate climates. Full sun, good drainage, frost hardy. Known as evening primrose as that is when the flowers are open.
perennial, herb	mauve	summer	leaves	Mediterranean to temperate climates. Full sun, moderate drainage, frost hardy. Leaves used for cookery.
shrub, evergreen	white	spring	flowers	Warm temperate climates. Full sun, good drainage, frost tender. Flowers are insignificant to look at but are extremely fragrant.
shrub, evergreen	white	autumn	flowers	Temperate climates. Full sun, good drainage, moderately frost hardy. Flowers are insignificant to look at but are extremely fragrant.
perennial, soft-wooded	mauve	spring to summer	leaves	Warm temperate climates. Full sun, good drainage, frost tender. Good groundcover or potted plant.
perennial, soft-wooded	mauve	spring to summer	leaves	Warm temperate climates. Full sun, good drainage, frost tender. Upright habit may need support.
perennial, soft-wooded	mauve	spring to summer	leaves	Warm temperate climates. Full sun, good drainage, frost tender. Sprawling growth habit makes a good groundcover.
biennial	white	summer	leaves	Mediterranean to temperate to subtropical climates. Full sun, moderate drainage. Popular culinary herb which self-seeds in suitable conditions.
shrub, evergreen	white	spring	leaves	Temperate climates. Full sun, perfect drainage, frost hardy. Foliage has spicy fragrance when crushed.

Botanic name	Common name	Family	Height x width	Plant type	Flower colour	Flowering time
Philadelphus coronarius	Mock orange	*Hydrangeaceae*	3 x 3m (10 x 10) ft	shrub, deciduous	white	spring
Philadelphus coronarius `Belle Etoile'	Mock orange	*Hydrangeaceae*	3 x 2.5 (10 x 8)	shrub, deciduous	white	spring
Philadelphus `Virginal'	Mock orange	*Hydrangeaceae*	3 x 2.5 (10 x 8)	shrub, deciduous	white	spring to summer
Pimpinella anisum	Anise	*Apiaceae*	0.1 x 0.1 (0.5 x 0.5)	annual	white	summer
Plumeria rubra	Frangipani	*Apocynaceae*	5-8 x 5 (16-25 x 16)	tree, deciduous	red to pink to white	summer
Polianthes tuberosa	Tuberose	*Amaryllidaceae*	1 x 0.1 (3 x 0.5)	tuber, deciduous	white	late summer to autumn
Populus balsamifera	Balsam poplar	*Salicaceae*	20-30 x 5 (65-100 x 16)	shrub, evergreen	greenish	spring to autumn
Populus trichocarpa	Black cottonwood	*Salicaceae*	30 x 20 (100 x 65)	tree, deciduous	reddish-purple	spring
Primula vulgaris	Common primrose	*Primulaceae*	0.1 x 0.1 (0.5 x 0.5)	perennial	yellow	spring
Prostanthera lasianthos	Victorian Christmas bush	*Lamiaceae*	3-5 x 2 (10-16 x 6)	tree, evergreen	white and purple	late spring to early summer
Prostanthera ovalifolia	Oval leafed mint bush	*Lamiaceae*	3 x 2 (10 x 6)	shrub, evergreen	purple	spring
Prostanthera rotundifolia	Round leafed mint bush	*Lamiaceae*	2.5 x 2 (8 x 6)	shrub, evergreen	mauve	spring
Prunus mume	Prunus	*Rosaceae*	6-8 x 4 (20 -25 x 13)	tree, deciduous	pink	winter
Rhododendron herzogi	Rhododendron	*Ericaceae*	3 x 2 (10 x 6)	shrub, evergreen	white-flushed pink	early spring
Rhododendron konori	Rhododendron	*Ericaceae*	1.5 x 1.5 (5 x 5)	shrub, evergreen	white-flushed pink	early spring
Rosa andrewsii	Scotch burnett rose	*Rosaceae*	1 x 0.5 (2 x 1.5)	shrub, deciduous	soft pink	spring
Rosa centifolia	Cabbage rose	*Rosaceae*	1.5 x 1 (5 x 3)	shrub, deciduous	pink	spring
Rosa damascena	Damask rose	*Rosaceae*	1.5 x 1 (5 x 3)	shrub, deciduous	clear pink	summer to autumn
Rosa damascena trigintipetala	Rose	*Rosaceae*	2 x 2 (6 x 6)	shrub, deciduous	pink	mid-summer
Rosa eglanteria	Briar rose	*Rosaceae*	2.5 x 1 (8 x 3)	shrub, deciduous	pink	late spring
Rosa gallica	French rose	*Rosaceae*	1 x 1 (3 x 3)	shrub, deciduous	pink	spring
Rosa primula	Rose	*Rosaceae*	2 x 2 (6 x 6)	shrub, deciduous	pale yellow	spring
Rosa 'Mme Alfed Carriere'	'Mme Alfred Carriere'	*Rosaceae*	6 x 5 (20 x 16)	climbing shrub, semi-evergreen	cream-blushed pink	spring to autumn
Rosa ' Constance Spry'	'Constance Spry'	*Rosaceae*	4 x 4 (13 x 13)	climbing shrub, deciduous	pink	early summer
Rosa 'Frau Dagmar Hastrup'	'Frau Dagmar Hastrup'	*Rosaceae*	1 x 1.5 (3 x 5)	shrub, deciduous	pale pink	spring
Rosa 'Blanc Double de Coubert'	'Blanc Double de Coubert'	*Rosaceae*	1.5 x 1 (5 x 3)	shrub, deciduous	white	spring to autumn
Rosa filipes 'Kiftsgate'	'Kiftsgate'	*Rosaceae*	10 x 3 (30 x 10)	climber, deciduous	white	summer

Fragrant parts	Preferred climate & growing notes & special uses
flowers	Mediterranean to cool temperate climates. Part-shade, good drainage, very frost hardy.
flowers	Mediterranean to cool temperate climates. Part-shade, good drainage, very frost hardy.
flowers	Mediterranean to cool temperate climates. Part-shade, good drainage, very frost hardy.
leaves	Warm temperate climates. Full sun, good drainage, frost tender. Licorice-scented leaves used in salads.
flowers	Warm temperate to subtropical and tropical climates. Full sun, good drainage, frost tender. Large branches can be struck as cuttings.
flowers	Temperate climates. Full sun, good drainage, moderately frost hardy. Clumps should be divided every 2-3 years. Wonderful cut flower.
buds & leaves	Cool temperate climates. Full sun, can tolerate poor drainage, very frost hardy. Roots are invasive of drains, buds are covered in perfumed balsam.
buds & leaves	Cool temperate climates. Full sun, can tolerate poor drainage, very frost hardy. Roots are invasive of drains, buds are covered in perfumed balsam.
flowers	Temperate climates. Part-shade, good drainage, frost hardy.
leaves	Cool temperate climates. Part-shade, good drainage, frost hardy. Prune lightly after flowering.
leaves	Temperate climates. Part-shade, good drainage, frost hardy. Prune lightly after fllowering.
leaves	Temperate climates. Part shade, good drainage, frost hardy. Prune lightly after flowering.
flowers	Cool temperate climates. Full sun, good drainage, frost hardy.
flowers	Warm temperate to subtropical climates. Part-sun, good drainage, frost tender. Forms a rounded shrub.
flowers	Temperate climates. Part sun, good drainage, frost tender. Has carnation-scented flowers and striking foliage with reddish new growth.
flowers	Mediterranean to temperate climates. Full sun, good drainage, frost hardy. Suckering shrub with brilliant autumn foliage and black heps. Good hedge plant.
flowers	Mediterranean to temperate climates. Full sun, good drainage, frost hardy.
flowers	Mediterranean to temperate climates. Full sun, good drainage, frost hardy.
flowers	Mediterranean to cool temperate climates. Full sun, good drainage, frost hardy. Flowers profusely.
flowers	Mediterranean to temperate climates. Full sun, good drainage, frost hardy. Arching branches, single blooms and bright red heps into winter.
flowers	Mediterranean to temperate climates. Full sun, good drainage, frost hardy. Suckering, low shrub with single blooms and stiff leathery leaves.
leaves	Mediterranean to temperate climates. Full sun, good drainage, frost hardy. Tiny aromatic leaves on long, arching branches.
flowers	Mediterranean to temperate climates. Full sun, good drainage, frost hardy. A vigorous climber with very few thorns and a long flowering season.
flowers	Mediterranean to temperate climates. Full sun, good drainage, frost hardy. Can be grown as a shrub or climber against a wall.
flowers	Mediterranean to temperate climates. Full sun, good drainage, frost hardy. Good hedging shrub with brilliant autumn foliage and colourful heips. Huge single blooms.
flowers	Mediterranean to temperate climates. Full sun, good drainage, frost hardy. Vigorous, hardy shrub for hedge or screen, good autumn foliage and red heps. Long flowering period.
flowers	Mediterranean to temperate climates. Full sun, good drainage, frost hardy. Vigorous with masses of single blooms with prominent gold stamens.

Prostanthera ovalifolia

Rosa eglanteria

Philadelphus coronarius

Rodney Hyett/Dale Harvey

121

'Mme Gregoire Stachelin'

The Source of Fragrance

*F*ragrance in plants come from the presence of essential oils (attars) in glands found in leaves (eucalyptus), bark (sassafrass trees), fruit (citrus rinds), wood (turpentine trees), seed (pepper trees), flowers (roses) and roots and underground stems (ginger).

Fragrance is created by the oils evaporating and molecules of it going into the air around us. Therefore, fragrance will be stronger as the temperature increases. If a flower has a very slight fragrance it can be intensified by putting the flower into a bag and leaving it in a warm place. Similarly, cutting flowers for the vase and then enclosing them in a confined space will also intensify the fragrance.

There are many different essential oils found in the plant kingdom and each one has its own characteristic smell; each plant will probably have a number of different compounds making up its complement of essential oils. Genetic make-up determines the oils carried by each species. Even within a species such as the rose each seedling born will vary in its oil content so that different varieties will be better than others in regard to fragrance.

Various terminology is used to describe fragance, such as scent for a delicate but pleasing smell, fragrance for a strong, pleasant smell, and odour for an unpleasant smell (such as the odour of rotting flesh which some flowers emit to attract blow-fly pollinators).

Botanic name	Common name	Family	Height x width
Rosa 'Kathleen Harrop'	'Kathleen Harrop'	Rosaceae	2 x 2m (6 x 6) ft
Rosa 'Zéphirine Drouhin'	'Zephirine Drouhin'	Roseaceae	4 x 2 (13 x 6)
Rosa 'Mme Sancy de Parabere'	'Mme Sancy de Parabere'	Roseaceae	4 x 2 (13 x 6)
Rosa 'Souvenir du Dr Jamain'	'Souvenir du Dr Jamain'	Rosaceae	2 x 2 (6 x 6)
Rosa 'Paul Neyron'	'Paul Neyron'	Rosaceae	2 x 1.5 (6 x 5)
Rosa 'Penelope'	'Penelope'	Rosaceae	1.5 x 1 (5 x 3)
Rosa 'Mme Hardy'	'Mme Hardy'	Rosaceae	1.5 x 1.5 (5 x 5)
Rosa 'Honorine de Brabant'	'Honorine de Brabant'	Rosaceae	2 x 1.5 (6 x 5)
Rosa 'Fantin Latour'	'Fantin Latour'	Rosaceae	1.5 x 1 (5 x 3)
Rosa 'Souvenir de la Malmaison'	'Souvenir de la Malmaison'	Rosaceae	2 x 2 (6 x 6)
Rosa rugosa 'Alba'	White rugosa	Rosaceae	2 x 2 (6 x 6)
Rosa multiflora	Briar rose	Rosaceae	3 x 3 (1 x 1)
Rosa 'Mme Gregoire Stachelin'	'Mme Gregoire Stachelin'	Rosaceae	5 x 3 (16 x 10)
Rosa 'Black Boy'	'Black Boy'	Rosaceae	2.5 x 1.5 (8 x 5)
Rosmarinus officinalis	Rosemary	Lamiaceae	1.5 x 1.5 (5 x 5)
Salvia officinalis	Sage	Lamiaceae	0.5 x 1 (1.5 x 3)
Satureja thymifolia	Savory of Crete	Lamiaceae	0.3 x 0.5 (1 x 1.5)
Schinus areria (syn S. molle)	Pepper tree	Anacardiaceae	10 x 5 (30 x 16)
Seneccio rowleyanus	String of beads	Asteraceae	trailer to 1m (3ft)
Sowerbaea juncea	Vanilla lily	Liliaceae	0.3 x 0.2 (1 x .5)
Spartium junceum	Spanish broom	Fabaceae	3 x 3 (10 x 6)
Stephanotis floribunda	Madagascar jasmine	Asclepiadaceae	depends on support
Sympthytum officinale	Comfrey	Boraginaceae	1 x 1 (3 x 3)
Syringa persica 'Laciniata'	Persian lilac	Oleaceae	3 x 2 (10 x 6)
Syringa vulgaris	Lilac	Oleaceae	3 x 2 (3 x 6)

Plant type	Flower colour	Flowering time	Fragrant parts	Preferred climate & growing notes & special uses
shrub, deciduous	pale pink	spring to autumn	flowers	Mediterranean to temperate climates. Full sun, good drainage, frost hardy. Thornless bush that can also be trained as a climber. Long flowering season.
shrub, deciduous	pink	summer to autumn	flowers	Mediterranean to temperate climates. Full sun, good drainage, frost hardy. Thornless bush or climber that flowers continuously through summer and autumn.
climber, deciduous	pink	mid-summer	flowers	Mediterranean to temperate climates. Full sun, good drainage, frost hardy. Thornless climber with lush leaves.
climber, deciduous	rich red	summer to autumn	flowers	Mediterranean to temperate climates. Full sun, good drainage, frost hardy. Protect from afternoon sun for best results.
shrub, deciduous	rich pink	spring	flowers	Mediterranean to temperate climates. Full sun, good drainage, frost hardy. One of the largest flowered roses; few thorns. Free flowering. Highly fragrant.
shrub, deciduous	cream-flushed pink	spring to autumn	flowers	Mediterranean to temperate climates. Full sun, good drainage, frost hardy. Suitable for hedges. Long flowering season followed by colourful heps.
shrub, deciduous	white	spring	flowers	Mediterranean to temperate climates. Full sun, good drainage, frost hardy. Healthy lush foliage and distinctive full blooms with green button eye.
shrub, deciduous	pink-striped	spring	flowers	Mediterranean to temperate climates. Full sun, good drainage, frost hardy. Strong growth which can be trained as a climber. Very few thorns.
shrub, deciduous	pink	spring	flowers	Mediterranean to temperate climates. Full sun, good drainage, frost hardy. Large, rounded, spreading shrub with handsome foliage.
shrub or climber, deciduous	pale pink	spring to autumn	flowers	Mediterranean to temperate climates. Full sun, good drainage, frost hardy. Highly double blooms with best display in autumn.
shrub, deciduous	white	spring to autumn	flowers	Mediterranean to temperate climates. Full sun, good drainage, frost hardy. Good for hedges with its lush green foliage and colourful heps.
shrub, evergreen	pink	spring	flowers	Mediterranean to temperate climates. Full sun, good drainage, frost hardy. Thornless, spreading shrub that can be used as a climber. Single blooms on long, arching canes.
climber, deciduous	pink	spring	flowers	Mediterranean to temperate climates. Full sun, good drainage, frost hardy. Large semi-double blooms. Good for pergolas and verandahs.
shrub or climber, deciduous	deep red	spring to autumn	flowers	Mediterranean to temperate climates. Full sun, good drainage, frost hardy. Pillar or climbing rose with large, very fragrant velvet black-red blooms.
shrub, evergreen	mauve to pink	spring to summer	leaves	Mediterranean to temperate climates. Full sun, good drainage, frost hardy. Leaves used for culinary purposes.
shrub, evergreen	mauve	summer	leaves	Mediterranean to temperate climates. Full sun, good drainage, frost hardy. Leaves used for culinary purposes.
perennial, herb	pink	summer	leaves & flowers	Mediterranean to temperate climates. Full sun, good drainage, frost hardy. Leaves used for culinary purposes.
tree, evergreen	white	spring to summer	leaves & fruit	Mediterranean to temperate to subtropical climates. Full sun, good drainage, frost tender. Beautiful weeping habit with attractive red berries in autumn..
evergreen, succulent	white	spring to autumn	flowers	Mediterranean to temperate climates. Full sun, good drainage, frost tender. Good for hanging baskets.
perennial, evergreen	purple	summer	flowers	Warm temperate climates. Full sun, moderate drainage, frost tender. Strong vanilla fragrance.Good as small tub plant.
shrub, deciduous	yellow	summer to early autumn	flowers	Mediterranean to temperate to subtropical climates. Full sun, good drainage, frost hardy. Prune lightly immediately after flowering.
climber, evergreen	white	spring to autumn	flowers	Warm temperature to subtropical and tropical climates. Part shade, good drainage, very frost tender. Very long flowering period. Good cut flower.
perennial, evergreen	pink	summer	leaves	Mediterranean to temperate climates. Part shade, moderate drainage, frost hardy. Can become invasive. Used as a medicinal herb.
shrub, deciduous	lilac	late spring to early summer	flowers	Cool temperate climates. Full sun, good drainage, very frost hardy. Needs a cold winter for best performance. Prune immediately after flowering.
shrub, deciduous	white to mauve to blue to pink	late spring to early summer	flowers	Cool temperate climates. Full sun, good drainage, very frost hardy. Needs a cold winter for best performance. Prune immediately after flowering.

Botanic name	Common name	Family	Height x width	Plant type	Flower colour	Flowering time
Tabernaemontana coronaria	See *Ervatamia*					
Tanacetum vulgare	Tansy	*Asteraceae*	1 x 1m *(3 x 3) ft*	perennial, herb	yellow	summer
Thuja occidentalis 'Rheingold'	American arbovitae	*Cupressaceae*	2 x 2 *(6 x 6)*	shrub, evergreen	n/a	n/a
Thymus praecox	Mother of thyme	*Lamiaceae*	0.05 x 1 *(0.2 x 3)*	perennial, evergreen	mauve	summer
Thymus serpyllum	Wild thyme	*Lamiaceae*	0.1 x 1 *(0.3 x 3)*	perennial, evergreen	pink	summer to autumn
Thymus vulgaris	Garden thyme	*Lamiaceae*	0.3 x 0.5 *(1 x 1.5)*	perennial, evergreen	mauve	summer to autumn
Thymus x citriodorus	Thyme golden lemon	*Lamiaceae*	0.1 x 0.3 *(0.3 x 1)*	perennial, evergreen	mauve	summer
Trachelospermum asiaticum		*Apocynaceae*	depends on support	climber, evergreen	cream ageing to yellow-white	spring to summer
Trachelospermum jasminoides	Star jasmine	*Apocynaceae*	depends on support	climber, evergreen	white	spring to summer
Tulipa saxatilis	Tulip	*Liliaceae*	0.3 x 0.1 *(1 x 0.3)*	bulb, deciduous	pink & yellow	spring
Viburnum x burkwoodii	Viburnum	*Caprifoliaceae*	2.5 x 2.5 *(8 x 8)*	shrub, semi-evergreen	pink then white	late winter to spring
Viburnum carlesii	Viburnum	*Caprifoliaceae*	2 x 2 *(6 x 6)*	shrub, deciduous	pink & white	late winter to spring
Viburnum fragrans (syn. farreri)	Viburnum	*Caprifoliaceae*	3 x 2 *(10 x 6)*	shrub, deciduous	pink & white	late winter to early spring
Viburnum x carlcephalum	Viburnum	*Caprifoliaceae*	2 x 2 *(6 x 6)*	shrub, deciduous	pink & white	spring
Viola odorata	Sweet violet	*Violaceae*	0.1 x 0.3 *(0.3 x 1)*	perennial, semi-evergreen	purple	late winter to early spring
Viola tricolor	Heartsease	*Violaceae*	0.1 x 0.1 *(0.3 x 0.3)*	annual or perennial	white, yellow & purple	spring to autumn
Virgilia oroboides (syn. capensis)	Cape virgilia	*Fabaceae*	8 x 6 *(25 x 20)*	large shrub, evergreen	pink	summer to autumn
Wisteria sinensis	Common wisteria	*Fabaceae*	depends on support	climber, deciduous	mauve to purple	spring
Wisteria floribunda	Japanese wisteria	*Fabaceae*	depends on support	climber, deciduous	mauve	early summer
Zieria species	Zieria	*Rutaceae*	1.5 x 2 *(5 x 6)*	shrub, evergreen	white to pink	spring

Wisteria floribunda

Wisteria sinensis

Viola tricolor

Fragrant parts	Preferred climate & growing notes & special uses
leaves	Mediterranean to temperate climates. Full sun, good drainage, frost hardy. Vigorous plant which spreads underground to form a clump. Good cut flower or dried flower.
leaves	Mediterranean to temperate climates. Full sun, good drainage, frost hardy. Compact conifer with nice gold colour and fragrant foliage.
leaves	Mediterranean to temperate climates. Full sun, good drainage, frost hardy. Used as a culinary herb.
leaves	Mediterranean to temperate climates. Full sun, good drainage, frost hardy. Used as a culinary herb.
leaves	Mediterranean to temperate climates. Full sun, good drainage, frost hardy. Used as a culinary herb.
leaves	Mediterranean to temperate climates. Full sun, good drainage, frost hardy. Used as a culinary herb.
flowers	Warm temperate to subtropical climates. Full sun, good drainage, frost tender.
flowers	Warm temperate to subtropical climates. Full sun, good drainage, frost tender. Long flowering period.
flowers	Cool temperate climates. Full sun, good drainage, frost hardy. Open, star-like flower shape.
flowers	Mediterranean to temperate climates. Full sun, good drainage, very frost hardy. Prune out old shoots after flowering.
flowers	Cool temperate climates. Full sun, good drainage, very frost hardy. Very strongly perfumed.
flowers	Cool temperate climates. Full sun, good drainage, frost hardy. Very strongly perfumed.
flowers	Cool temperate climates. Full sun, good drainage, very frost hardy. Very strongly perfumed.
flowers	Mediterranean to temperate climates. Part-shade, good drainage, frost hardy. Clumps can be easily divided to multiply plants.
flowers	Mediterranean to temperate climates. Part-shade, good drainage, frost hardy.
flowers	Mediterranean to temperate climates. Full sun, good drainage, frost hardy. Fast growing but short-lived. Good screen plant.
flowers	Mediterranean to temperate climates. Full sun, good drainage, frost hardy. Very vigorous, roots can cause problems near buildings. Short flowering period.
flowers	Mediterranean to temperate climates. Full sun, good drainage, frost hardy. Much longer flower heads than common Wisteria and not as invasive a root system.
leaves	Temperate climates. Full sun, perfect drainage, moderately frost hardy. Foliage has an interesting spicy fragrance when crushed.

Thymus vulgaris

Viburnum burkwoodii

Cordyline Australis

Interesting Foliages

The cabbage tree (Cordyline Australis) is an unusual plant, much favoured by colonial gardeners and is still used by gardeners who like a strong architectural accent. A palm-like shrub it has sharp leaves and sweetly fragrant spikes of tiny white flowers in late spring.

String of Beads (Senecia rowleyanus) is an indoor plant that attracts attention. A perennial succulent suited to growing in hanging baskets or pots, it has fragrant white flowers from summer to winter and trailing stems of bead-like green leaves.

Another Australian native with a particular quirk is the chocolate lily (Dichopogon fimbriatus). It has grass-like leaves and mauve flowers with a distinctive chocolate fragrance which perfumes the air throughout summer.

Rodney Hyett/Dale Harvey/Andre Martin

Index

127